WARRIOR ENTREPRENEUR

Mr Rogers,

Thank you

for all you

do to inspire

our next generation

of warriors

ZACH

WARRIOR ENTREPRENEUR

LESSONS FROM THE BATTLEFIELD TO THE BOARDROOM

ZACHARY L. GREEN

NEW DEGREE PRESS

COPYRIGHT © 2021 ZACHARY L. GREEN

WARRIOR ENTREPRENEUR

Lessons from the Battlefield to the Boardroom

ISBN   978-1-63730-583-6 *Paperback*
        978-1-63730-584-3 *Kindle Ebook*
        978-1-63730-585-0 *Ebook*

CONTENTS

———

DEDICATION

———

I used to think that behind every warrior was a strong female warrior. As I have walked my warrior journey, I realize that is not true. They are not behind the warrior. Sometimes they are next to the warrior; many times they are in front of the warrior encouraging them to conquer their crucibles and accomplish the mission no matter how hard they may be tested.

My warrior hero is my wife Dr. Jennifer Green. On our very first date, I remember her asking me why I joined the US Marine Corps. I remember enthusiastically telling her it was because I loved the challenge. I loved being part of an elite team. I loved the connection to the USMC warriors of the past like Dan Daly, Chesty Puller, and Smedtly Butler. I spoke about the mission of the Marine Corps as the tip of the spear of our military and the protectors of freedom. The more I waxed poetically about why I joined my beloved Corps, the more she smiled. After I spoke, she said, "Interesting, those are all the reasons I became a physician." I knew right there, on our first date, I had met my fellow warrior, my soulmate, my bashert טרעששאַב.

Over the almost twenty-five years since that first date, she has shown me what grace under pressure looks like. She has reminded me life is not what happens to you but rather how you react to it. She has been dealt many overwhelming challenges that would destroy a mere mortal. They ranged from life-threatening illnesses, hostile work environments, and loss of her mother, father, and sister all in a few years' time. As she was tried and tested during these times of challenge, she always put my son and me first and carried on the best she knew how. When I was in the middle of my personal crucibles, she was the one encouraging me to be brave and to be bold and would always remind me with her gentle words of encouragement like "you can do it" and "I believe in you." She was my voice when I couldn't speak. She was the light that lifted me out of the dark struggles of my warrior journey. I dedicate this book to her and all the female warriors who make the world a better place.

INTRODUCTION

Warrior. Such a visual word. It can bring up images of knights, amazons, ninjas, and Maori. These people were fighting literal battles that could be clearly won or lost. However, there are other types of warriors—successful people who find their way into happiness and fulfillment after overcoming obstacles. For them, the world resembles nothing short of a battleground, and they fight challenge after challenge to become the best version of themselves.

You see it in their eyes, their body language.

You feel it in their presence.

They have fought their battles and done so bravely.

This book is about warriors who battled their way through attacks, fought adversity, and accepted every challenge that came their way. We take a deep dive into what makes a warrior a warrior. We look at the common principles and actions that separate warriors from the common man. We take a look at adversity and how adversity makes the warrior learn and grow. Adversity is a common theme with most warriors—it is the resistance that encourages growth and transformation. While others may want to avoid adversity, a warrior views adversity as a necessary part of growth. Finally, a warrior doesn't always appear as a muscle-bound Spartan or knight in shining armor. A warrior can be found in the halls of a start-up incubator, working on their laptop in a coffee shop, or even in the garage turned into an entrepreneur's first office. It is the spirit of the warrior that we will investigate and highlight. It is the common themes that we will unpack and explore in the pages to come. The goal of this book is to use these stories, research, and examples to unlock the inner warrior in you.

Courage is not the absence of fear but rather meeting fear head on. In the early days of my entrepreneurial journey, I knew the easy path was to quit and give up; the hard path was to keep going. That is the warrior's path, to fight on through the difficult times and never give up. I could never let down my investors, vendors, and employees. I was on a mission, and a warrior always completes his mission.

All the adversity I've had in my life, all my troubles and obstacles, have strengthened me. You may not realize it when it happens, but a kick in the teeth may be the best thing in the world for you.

—WALT DISNEY

The awards and recognition only come if you follow a few simple steps. To be successful, especially when it comes to business and entrepreneurship, you need to embrace adversity as a way to grow and learn. All of your hardships sharpen your thought processes, as they did for me when I created an award-winning multi-million-dollar company that started with a simple idea to help out my fellow firefighters who would become disorientated in the dark and smoke-filled battlefield of a structure fire. One idea led to another as I celebrated the successes and learned from my failures. I often didn't think I could make it, but the lessons I learned as a US Marine, firefighter, and warrior entrepreneur prepared me for the battles that lay ahead. Today, my company has made tens of millions of dollars, our products are used by over 100,000 firefighters from over twenty-five countries, our safety products are sold by major retailers such as The Home Depot, and I was even asked to testify in front of the US House of Representatives Small Business Committee. I stand today as a warrior entrepreneur, and I would like to share my story and the story of other warriors be it from the battlefield to the boardroom. This book will focus on the common themes that make you grow and learn: adversity, grit, and the never give up mindset.

Strength does not come from winning.
Your struggles develop your strengths.
When you go through hardships and
decide not to surrender, that is strength.

—ARNOLD SCHWARZENEGGER

In this book, I will talk about the many warriors of today and throughout history who were never afraid to face tough times. We will look at some examples of these warriors and their stories, and learn from their resilience and how adversity made them grow and learn. These accounts of their strength, willpower, and desire to prevail against all odds are what unlock the warrior in all of us.

A warrior's journey typically has a point at which you are tested unlike anything you have ever experienced in your life. A crucible, an event that tests the soul. It is at the crucible that the warrior chooses to fail and quit or to dig deep and realize that a transformation has to happen to continue their mission. The crucible can occur in the early phases of training, and it can happen again in the execution of your mission. It is at this terrifying point that a warrior is made.

A crisis of faith, a crisis of existence, a crisis of what you believed to be true up to this point in your life is what pushes you forth. This is typically the most pivotal juncture in a warrior's life. This where you realize everything you believe in, everything that has gotten you where you are now, is not enough. Here is when you look into the abyss and realize that to make it to the next stage of your mission, you have to disconnect from your past, shed your former self, and transform.

At this moment, you take a personal inventory. The warrior has to take the mental scars, bad relationships, self-doubt, bad habits, and fear and let them be consumed by the abyss. Although you try to put that chaos in order, you will realize it is in the chaos you grow, learn, and transform into a true warrior. The warrior sees clarity in the chaos, the warrior stands tall in the face of that chaos and inspires others to be their best self.

An old African proverb says, "Smooth seas do not make skillful sailors." You need this critical moment in your life, as well as the training that prepares you to truly grow, adapt, and overcome. An entrepreneur has to follow this same transformational journey. In most cases, an entrepreneur leaves the safety of a traditional job and the cubicle farm to embark on their entrepreneurial venture. They have to follow the warrior's way. When they meet their crucible and stare into their abyss, they realize what is most important. That's when they find their "why."

CHAPTER 1

FIGHTING THROUGH THE ABYSS

———

"Tell the story of the mountain you climbed. Your words could become a page in someone else's survival guide."
—MORGAN HARPER NICHOLS

BREATHE! You've got to breathe, Zach!

I am literally dying as I try to breathe.

My lungs have been ravaged by COVID-19 over the last ten days. What started as some nausea after being exposed to the coronavirus has now progressed to COVID-19 double lung pneumonia and has damaged my lungs to the point of debilitating difficulty in breathing.

The room starts to fill with more and more medical personnel as they move around with focused attention like dancers in a ballet.

Some of the staff hovers over me with bright lights. I can feel various tubes and machines forcing air into my lungs. I can hear them talk about the availability of a ventilator and if there is space in the ICU for me. As I fight for my next breath, the blackness starts to block out the light in the room.

I can't do it.

I try to find the rhythm to allow my lungs to fill with air, but I just can't fight to breathe anymore. The darkness of the abyss in front of me starts to come into focus. It is deep and dark, and it is pulling me downward. It's not the beautiful light at the end of the tunnel many people talk about when they come to the end of their life. The bright white light of the peaceful pathway to the other side is not there.

I am looking at pure nothingness, a darkness blacker than black, a bottomless pit whose emptiness is pulling me down this black tunnel.

This is my story about igniting the warrior inside me, the warrior who's in all of us. The warrior who overcomes our personal crucibles. The warrior who enters the abyss, fights through what made them get pulled into the event horizon of our personal black holes and come out the other side victorious and stronger. This book is a collection of lessons, research, and stories from and about warriors who come in many forms and are found in many places. From the battle-field to the boardroom to the entrepreneurial start-up halls. This book will take you through lessons on what makes a warrior different. A warrior doesn't have to be clad in armor or kitted out in military tactical gear.

A warrior can be a single mother struggling to start up her business while working two part-time jobs.

A warrior could be an entrepreneur who poured their blood, sweat, and tears into their business only to see it almost fail. The common trait of a warrior is the indelible drive for success and mission accomplishment.

A warrior is someone who never gives up and always gives it their all to accomplish their mission.

A warrior is someone who embraces adversity as a learning opportunity, not as something that should be avoided. This is the story of how I became a warrior and learned from other warriors about the invincible spirit and how I used that to fight through almost dying from COVID-19.

Two weeks prior in December of 2020, I had contracted COVID-19. I'd been very vigilant about masking up indoors and maintaining social distancing, but at home, I felt like I was safe. I had a few fellow Marines over at my house working on an all-day project several weeks before. We all felt invincible, but obviously we weren't, and this invisible little virus was stealthily infecting us in the sanctity of my home as we left our masks off and didn't maintain distance.

The next day, I started feeling a bit queasy, and by the third day, I couldn't get out of bed.

The next week brought the most intense nausea and chills I have ever experienced. I stopped eating and drinking.

Finally, the delirium set in, and I found myself on the floor being picked up by the life squad. I made it to the hospital and spent most of the next few hours on a stretcher in the hallway, as all rooms were taken.

It was at this point my breathing started to fail. Thankfully, several of my fellow firefighters were on medic duty and recognized me in the hallway. They were able to get me the immediate attention I so desperately needed. They are my brother and sister warriors and they, like all warriors, always take care of our fellow warriors.

I couldn't generate enough oxygen as COVID-19 had diminished my lung's ability to absorb oxygen. They started increasing my external oxygen from two liters up to ten liters with no real change in my condition. Eventually they moved me to a room with twenty-four-hour monitoring as my oxygen level kept failing even with the increase of sixty liters of forced O_2.

The next night my coughing became violent, and I realized I was choking and suffocating. My O_2 levels were in the sixties. I couldn't reach the emergency nurse's call button. I thought I was going to die in a room by myself. Finally, a nurse came in followed by about eight other specialists. They were preparing to intubate me but finally the advanced oxygen rebreather started to bring up my oxygen levels.

For the last several days I had laid on my stomach in the COVID-19 isolation floor. This is where all of the COVID-19 patients have been quarantined with around-the-clock care and monitoring.

I hadn't eaten in over twelve days.

I was lying half-naked on my stomach sweating and delirious with heart monitors, IVs, and tubes surrounding every part of my body to the point I couldn't even roll over. No visitors were permitted. Any staff who came into the room looked like an astronaut covered in protective gear and breathing contraptions. I'm a very social person and I can't stand being alone, and at my darkest moment, I found myself without my family and friends at a time I needed them most.

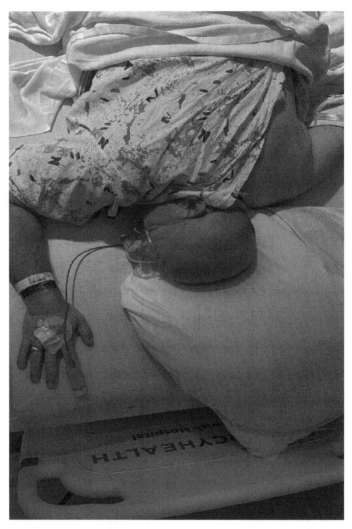

Author Zachary Green in the COVID Unit of Jewish Hospital-Kenwood (Cincinnati, Ohio)

My thoughts were consumed with how I would be able to take that next elusive breath. I could feel myself falling to the bottom of the abyss each time I struggled to find my next breath. At times when I was struggling to breathe and the delirium of not eating or getting enough oxygen would set in, I could feel myself looking down on myself. I could literally see myself as I floated above my body.

I had fought so hard over the last few days I had virtually nothing physically, mentally, or even spiritually left in me to fight with. If I could have just given up and fallen to the bottom of that dark abyss, maybe the respirator would be waiting for me. Being intubated and having the respirator breathe for me would give me the desperate break I needed. Just slightly repositioning myself caused me to suffocate. For several days, I had to stay still so I could exhale and inhale perfectly in order to capture and receive each breath. I've never realized how sacred and delicate the mere act of breathing is. It is the constant gift of life so easy to take for granted each time we inhale and exhale. Without breath, we die, yet we never think of that. We just live our days never thinking this magical gift of nourishing breath.

Earlier in the week, a respiratory therapist told me if I can't bring in enough oxygen through my breathing in the next few days, they would have to intubate me and put me into a medically induced coma. I later found out that there is a 35.7 percent mortality rate for COVID-19 patients who are intubated and have to surrender to the ventilator. He told me I needed to avoid this at all costs as the longer you are intubated, the more difficult it eventually is to have your lungs function on their own. Bottom line was there would be a significant chance I will soon die if I can't breathe on my own right now. I know that giving up at this point would be the easy thing to do, but I also know I am a warrior and a US Marine.

Once a Marine, always a Marine. Marines NEVER GIVE UP.

As a US Marine and firefighter, I have previously faced death several times in my life but nothing so visceral and intimate as what I had gone through over those days in that hospital room.

In the military and fire service, there is an expectation to battle lethal forces and operate in life-threatening conditions. That's part of the job. However, you almost always have a team with you. That team is supported by the knowledge gained from centuries of lessons and refined doctrine. You can pretty much plan for most of what you know will come. You practice over and over until your team moves as one. When chaos starts, everyone has a job to do, and we work together like a flowing unit. Using tools, gear, and time-honed tactics and maneuvers, we meet the enemy and then defeat it.

This is a very different battle. There is virtually no history to learn from when it comes to COVID-19. There is a lot of trial and error. I don't have my rifle, my knife, or my combat gear ready for this fight. I didn't have my fellow Marines with me. I didn't have my fire truck and fellow firefighting crew. My PPE (personal protective equipment), the fire protective gear made of Kevlar and Nomex, were missing. The protection from my firefighter helmet, the firefighting weapon of my trusted axe, and a fire hose were not with me.

This time, I'm facing the ultimate battle with death by myself in a hospital bed, on my stomach, practically naked.

But in this fight, my fellow combat warriors have been replaced by an incredible team of medical heroes. The nurses, doctors, and medical specialists helped me stay alive with the tools of knowledge, science, and technology. They move around the room with focus, dedication, and purpose. Over the last few days, whenever I lost consciousness, they yelled at me that I needed to breathe. They held my hand, rubbed my back, and provided both the medical and the emotional support I needed to find that next breath. It was the nursing team at Jewish Hospital of Kenwood (Cincinnati, Ohio) who helped me channel my warrior spirit and allowed me to battle back from the abyss. I owe my life to nurses Chris Pinkerton, Akiko Apling, Walt Scott, Scott Critclow, Christina Vest, and my firefighting brother Eric who took such good care of me.

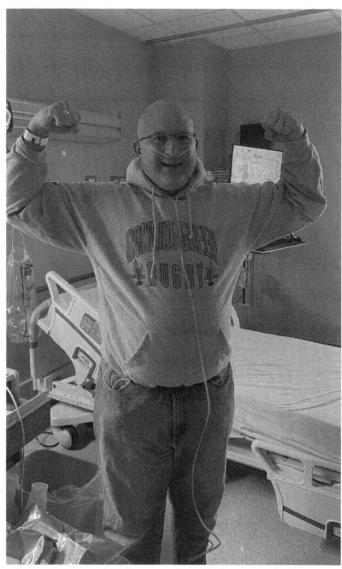

Author Zachary Green being discharged after almost two weeks of hospitalization due to COVID-19 double lung pneumonia

As you read through the following pages you will find research on the history of warriors, the neuroscience behind fight or flight, and how adversity makes you grow. I will highlight dozens of warriors, from Navy SEALs to ancient Spartans to Naval Aviators.

In addition to these types of combat warriors, we will also dive into lessons from warrior entrepreneurs and business leaders focusing on the common warrior theme they all share.

Throughout the book, I will also share stories from my journey of starting my company out of the trunk of my car and growing it into a multi-million-dollar business whose customers range from The Home Depot to Kroger to the US government and close to 100,000 firefighters from over twenty-five countries.

It is my hope that the lessons and inspiration gained from the following pages inspire the warrior in all of us.

CHAPTER 2

MY STORY

———

Life for a child with attention and learning disorders is quite a challenge. In fact, 51.5 percent of children with ADHD have behavioral or conduct problems. School is hard. Making and maintaining friends is hard. Seeing others easily succeed while you struggle is hard. Trying to please your family is hard. This was the case with me, as well.

I attended five schools between kindergarten and twelfth grade. I was the perfect picture of a kid with learning disabilities caused by ADHD and dyslexia—you could find me reading a book, watching TV, throwing spit wads at the back of the teacher, and telling a joke all at the same time. I was always in motion both physically and mentally.

Roger Bacon High School, St. Bernard (Cincinnati) Ohio

My mind wandered, and I spent a lot of time in detention and getting in trouble, feeling like a failure. I look back now and recognize ADHD is just another word for multitasking, which is now a positive skillset in my life.

I consider being called an energetic and multitasking executive as a compliment. Those same traits exhibited by a kid in school of being hyper and not being able to stick to one task at a time is regarded as a learning disability. School, for me, was a constant challenge as I tried to channel my energy and focus. My parents were completely supportive and moved me to different schools that offered programs and the support structure I needed to help me successfully learn and grow. Montessori schools, public schools, and private schools all seemed like they were forcing me to fit a round peg into a square hole.

It wasn't until I ended up at a Franciscan-run Catholic school named Roger Bacon High School in Cincinnati that I started to see how discipline, integrity, and the warrior spirit of our mascot, the Spartans, could finally allow me to achieve the success I always knew I was destined for. Without the love and support of my parents, teachers, coaches, and the staff of Roger Bacon High School, I know I wouldn't be where I am today. They saw my potential and turned my challenges into opportunities, which helped me see my disabilities as abilities, thereby developing them into strengths.

THE UNITED STATES MARINE CORPS

I always had a deep love and appreciation for my country and was obsessed with the US Marine Corps even at a very young age. While the other kids in the neighborhood played soccer and rode their bikes, I was spreading mud on my face and crawling through the woods with a stick as my imaginary gun, reenacting great Marine Corps battles such as Belleau Woods and Iwo Jima. I tried to sign up for the Marines when I was eight years old. Instead, they gave me a poster of a US Marine Corps infantryman decked out with camouflage, M-16 rifle, and Ka-Bar knife, and told me to come back ten years later. That poster stayed on my wall over the next decade as my inspiration to one day become a Marine Corps warrior.

Within hours of my eighteenth birthday, I walked into the US Marine recruiting station in the Mt. Healthy (Cincinnati, Ohio) Gold Circle shopping center and met Sergeant Beatry Huston. Sgt. Huston looked just like the Marine in the recruiting poster. His big chest, small waist, and infectious confidence topped off with perfect posture greeted me when I walked in his office. He looked at me and asked why I was there. Even though I always knew I would become a Marine, I also wanted to see what the other branches offered. In an effort to try and make him jealous and "sweeten up the pot," I told him the Army offered me a big signing bonus, the Air Force told me about all the technical skills I would learn, and the Navy told me about the adventures I would have sailing the seven seas.

I asked him what the Marine Corps could offer me. I could tell this question deeply bothered him. His smile turned to a grimace, and he barked, "NOTHING!" He stated that the USMC was one of the greatest fighting forces in the history of the world, and it would continue to be that way with or without me. He stated that the real question was what I could offer the Marines. He finally concluded by saying he didn't think I was tough enough to even make it through boot camp at Parris Island.

As he spoke, I heard my teachers' voices telling me I wasn't good enough, and I decided it was time for me to stand up to those who didn't know the real me and what I was capable of doing and accomplishing. I grabbed the contract out of his hand, signed it on the spot, and before I knew it, I was standing on the yellow footprints of Marine Corps Recruit Depot at Parris Island, SC.

The infamous yellow footprints, Marine Corps Recruit Depot, Parris Island, SC

One of the most miserable places known to man. As I walked through those polished silver hatches (doors) I looked above me and saw in gold letters, "THROUGH THESE PORTALS PASS PROSPECTS FOR AMERICA'S FINEST FIGHT

FORCE UNITED STATES MARINES." I had no idea how the next few months would so drastically change my life.

Receiving Building, Marine Corps Recruit Depot, Parris Island, SC

Marine Corps recruit training is brutal. The only thing harsher than the superhuman drill instructors was the relentless heat, humidity, and constant bites of the evil and invisible sand fleas. I was pushed physically, mentally, and emotionally further and harder than I could have ever imagined.

As the weeks of boot camp progressed, I struggled. I had never been challenged so hard. I was at my personal breaking point, and I could feel the pull of wanting to give up. It all finally came to a head on the hot asphalt of the main parade deck when one of the drill instructors singled me out for

IPT (incentive physical training)—calisthenics designed to punish.

Imagine a superhuman drill instructor screaming at you to do push-ups until your arms gave out, and before you had a chance to rest, he would then make you switch to sit-ups. As your stomach started to cramp, he would then switch to "bends and thrusts," a brutal combination of dropping to the push-up position, then jumping up as high as you can and then back to the push up position. This process would continue over and over as you would become both disoriented and severely out of breath. At some point, I wasn't able to keep up with his commands, and I started to struggle. Finally, I collapsed to the ground and started to cry. I had hit my mental and physical wall. I literally felt myself become absorbed by the abyss of my self-pity and failure.

He bent over my shivering body, and calmly said, "I always knew you were a quitter; I always knew you didn't have what it takes to be a Marine. Your mommy and daddy aren't here to help you anymore." His words cut deeply, and my tears developed into uncontrollable sobs. Although it was his deep and gruff voice that said those crushing words, I also heard the voices of teachers and others who had said similar things during my short life span of eighteen years.

At that point, I transformed. I decided no matter what anyone said to me, no matter how anyone treated me or judged me, I was going to prove all of them wrong. I resolved that I was destined for greatness, and no one would ever stand in the way of me changing the world. I climbed out of that abyss of self-doubt and despair, and the fire that drill instructor ignited in me that day helped me realize what is at the heart of the Marine Corps warrior spirit: mission accomplishment. I took that developed drive at enlisted recruit training at Parris Island and used it to graduate at the top in my platoon at Officer's Candidate School in Quantico, VA, a few years later.

PFC Zachary Green, Official Marine Corps Recruit Depot Portrait, Parris Island, SC

LCpl Zachary Green, Marine Corps Air Ground Combat Center, Twentynine Palms, CA

After close to nine years of service as an US Marine, I made the decision to not reenlist and to continue to serve my country as a civilian. Although my original goal was to serve as an officer in the US Marines until retirement, I decided I would rather explore other areas in the civilian arena. I had just met the love of my life, and she gave me the old ultimatum: "It's either me or the Corps…" Needless to say, my decision has turned out to be a wise one, as there is no way I would have been able to achieve this level of success and happiness without her by my side.

Still, a few years and fifty pounds later, I struggled with an emptiness and loss of purpose in my civilian life. I felt that fire to serve and be part of a group of warriors. I needed something to reignite the warrior in me.

The day was September 11, 2001, a day the world changed. That day, most of us remember exactly where we were when we saw those planes turn into missiles as they slammed into the World Trade Tower Twin Towers and the Pentagon. It was a day that ignited the warrior in all of us as we realized for the first time in our nation's history that the battlefield was no longer in a far-off, distant land but was in our own backyard.

I felt compelled to take action too and do something that would forever change my life trajectory and set me on an adventure I could have never imagined; I joined my local volunteer fire department so I could continue to serve my community. Even though it was different from the Marine Corps, it still had the same intangibles of warrior service but with a little more enjoyment. The Marine Corps had the special gift of taking things that should be very fun and making them as miserable as possible, whereas the fire department had a way of making miserable things seem as fun as possible. I couldn't be with my Marine Corps brothers and sisters to take the fight to our nation's enemies while I went to work in my suit and tie as a civilian. I had to get back to the battlefield; I had to serve my country again. My inner warrior was fighting to be unleashed. This time, though, the front lines of the war were no longer in a far-off land. The front lines were our neighborhoods and communities. I signed up with the local fire department of hometown of Wyoming, Ohio, just outside of Cincinnati. I once again had the privilege and honor of serving a cause bigger than myself.

FIREFIGHTING

Fire Lieutenant Zachary Green, Wyoming Fire Department, Wyoming (Cincinnati), Ohio

When I became a volunteer firefighter, my full-time job was in the pharmaceutical industry for Eli Lilly. I worked in many roles, from field sales to sales management to training and strategy and development. However, my passion was in brand marketing, which is where I learned the value of building and growing a brand around solving a problem.

My career has always been in helping people solve problems. During my time in sales, I realized what makes a product great isn't the features or the high-end packaging; it is simply the fact that it **solves a problem**. Any product that solves a problem is very likely to be successful. However, I found some of the greatest value was when people looked up to you as a trusted advisor because you showed them they could solve a problem they didn't even know they had. These lessons didn't just help me in my career in sales, but also throughout my life.

As a firefighter, I had a life-changing experience early in my career during a live-fire training exercise. I lost my way in a building when I found myself in a walk-in closet and became dangerously disoriented. The conditions were very dark, and I could barely see a few feet in front of me. I thought I was in a hallway and knew that hallways typically lead to steps that lead to the way out. However, I couldn't find a door or steps, I was boxed in by the three walls at the back of a walk-in closet. I panicked. I looked down at my remaining air on the regulator gauge and knew I only had a few minutes left until my air supply would be critically low. I was lost, I was disorientated, and I was scared. Darkness brings a primal fear that cuts deeper than the learned fear we have from movies and books. I fought through that fear and remembered my training of what we should do when we get lost in a structure fire. I was able to find the hose and follow it back to the fire engine/pumper outside.

> "Courage is not the absence of fear, but the triumph over it. The brave man is not he who does not feel afraid, but he who conquers that fear."
>
> —NELSON MANDELA

When I got outside, I shared my experience with my captain, and he kind of laughed off my concerns and fear as he explained this loss of visibility in a dark and smoky building is just something that happens, and I would have to "work through it," just as all firefighters before me have done. That really didn't sit well with me. Although I heard everything he said to me, I couldn't accept it. I knew there had to be a better way to solve this common problem of being disoriented in the dark.

MY ENTREPRENEURIAL JOURNEY

> Just as we develop our physical muscles through overcoming opposition—such as lifting weights—we develop our character muscles by overcoming challenges and adversity.
>
> —STEPHEN COVEY

I started researching ways to help firefighters reduce disorientation and increase accountability in the dark battleground created by heavy black smoke. I wanted to help my brother and sister firefighters see each other and their tools in the dark so they could have a visual light reference point in the dark that would make them safer in these disorienting conditions.

I used this terrifying experience in that burning building along with my warrior attitude of using adversity as a learning tool, and I developed something that could help solve this problem—one that has affected so many other firefighters and others in the dark. This "something" would be the start of my journey as an entrepreneur. I worked with some very creative scientists, developers, and engineers to produce a high-output photoluminescent technology (think of it as glow-in-the-dark on steroids) that could be embedded in various firefighter items such as helmet accessories and tools that would make them "glow" in the dark.

This glow would thereby increase visibility and reduce disorientation for firefighters in the dark and smoke. The light from the glow would create a visual reference point in what would usually be nothing but darkness. These life-saving products would help firefighters do their job better, more efficiently, and, most of all, safely. After considerable testing and real-world trials, I ended up with a working prototype made out of high-temperature-resistant silicone that could be placed on top of the brim of a firefighter's helmet.

A few weeks later, we had a structure fire. As I was crawling down a dark and smoke-filled hallway, I felt someone grab my helmet. As I turned around to see what was happening, the bright green glow reflected from my helmet band illuminated the wide-eyed expression of amazement on my fellow firefighter's face behind his facemask. He wanted to find out what was lighting up my helmet, and I wanted to get the "wet stuff" on the "red stuff" and extinguish the fire.

After the fire was extinguished, we were loading the hoses back on the fire engine. Everyone kept talking about the bright green glow around my fire helmet so visible in the dark interior of the house. Before I knew it, my fellow firefighters were asking me if I could make them one. They were throwing twenty-dollar bills for their helmet bands faster than I could write down their names.

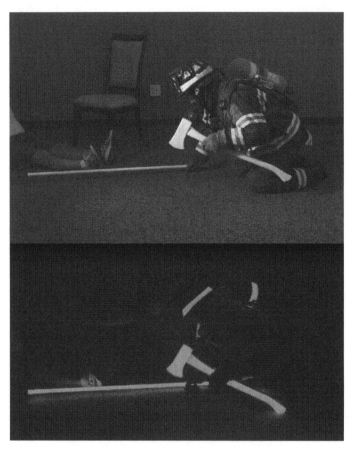

Foxfire® Illuminating Firefighting Products in use

I first had to think about how I could brand and market this new idea. I landed on the name MN8® for this new company because the glow was so bright it "em-an-ated" light. Under that new company, I named the brand Foxfire® in homage to the bioluminescent Foxfire mushroom used to illuminate the inside of the Revolutionary War submarine called the Turtle.

The responses from fellow firefighters, when they saw how visible I was in the dark, was both a literal and figurative green light to further develop this product line. The successful impact of this helmet band started me on a trajectory of developing other glow in the dark firefighting accessories and products that would eventually grow to a line used by close to 100,000 firefighters in over twenty-five countries. My first step in this entrepreneurial journey was to see if I could make a viable sales model out of selling these glow-in-the-dark products for firefighters. I started selling them out of the trunk of my car, traveling from fire station to fire station in my free time.

My conversations with my fellow firefighters centered on how the problem of being lost in the dark could be solved with this energy-free lighting technology rather than just selling the features of the specific products. I would usually have to go into an area that was completely dark to show them how the products glowed. Typically, the only place in a fire station that was dark enough was the bathroom, as they typically didn't have windows. My conversations usually would start with, "Hi, my name is Zach, and I'm a firefighter from the Cincinnati area. Can we all go in the bathroom together, turn out the light, and then I can show you something really cool…?" Well, a line like that usually gets attention and if they didn't immediately throw me out of the station, they would usually follow me into that dark bathroom and buy everything I brought with me. These products were quite a hit, and I made close to $5,000 over the course of six months. This was a huge win for me because it let me know people were willing to pay me for a product that solved the problem firefighters have experienced since they started interior fire-fighting operations.

When the sales of these glow in the dark products began to grow, I had an epiphany. Everything that I had ever learned from my varied experiences—including my time in the US Marines, as a sales professional, and then my experience in the pharmaceutical companies—came together and helped me become an entrepreneur. I was not only solving a problem, but I was also on a mission to help those who protect us. I was becoming an entrepreneur, the realization of my childhood dream.

I'll never forget the moment when I made up my mind to quit my job at Eli Lilly and go all in on becoming an entrepreneur. My fire chief, Robert Rielage, sat me down at his office one day and started to share a story with me about how we all have a life mission. He said this could be my life's mission and nothing could be nobler than helping heroes do their job better and safer. He said this concept I had been working on for the last several months had the opportunity to change the firefighting industry as we knew it.

As I walked out of his office, I remembered the words of one of my favorite leaders, President Theodore Roosevelt: "In any moment of decision, the best thing you can do is the right thing, the next best thing is the wrong thing, and the worst thing you can do is nothing." All the challenges I had faced and overcome helped me create something that would both help me grow a company and keep our heroes safer, as well as those they protect. As word of mouth spread and sales started to accelerate, I invested more money in this business.

I eventually refinanced my home, maxed out my credit cards, and even borrowed from my retirement savings to help build inventory and structure the business for growth. I saw true potential, and everyone around me saw the same, but I had no idea the risks, sacrifices, and adversity I would experience to realize that potential.

Six months later, I took these products to the FDIC (Fire Department Instructor's Conference) trade show. This was the largest firefighter trade show in the USA, with over 40,000 firefighters in one place. This would be a real-life indicator as to whether I could expand the business from selling out of the trunk of my car to seeing if large departments and distributors saw enough value in the solutions these products provided. More importantly, I could find out whether they were willing to make department-wide purchases and carry inventory thereby helping me grow the company.

Our small booth was surrounded by multi-billion-dollar companies whose booths cost hundreds of thousands of dollars. Our booth was a modest black soccer tent held together with duct tape and zip ties to create a blacked-out environment that could showcase how our glow in the dark products reduced disorientation and increased accountability. I had my brother firefighters, Peter, Buck, and Buck's sister Ayrie help in the booth with me, and they also shared their experiences of how these products helped them. Unlike the other companies who were large corporations making money from firefighters, we were one of them. We were a company of firefighters for firefighters.

As the show progressed, we became the talk of the attendees. Each hour our booth became more crowded, and eventually we had a line waiting to come into our booth that extended past the sparkly populated booths of the large corporations. Our booth was so busy and so crowded we had a hard time just taking in all the money from the lines of firefighters wanting to buy our products. We ended up booking almost $100,000 in sales in three days!

We had a problem, though. We didn't have enough raw materials or the infrastructure to fill all those orders. But a warrior doesn't back down from a challenge. A warrior improvises, overcomes, and adapts. I was going to do whatever it took to fill these orders. My first challenge was to find more money to buy additional raw materials to begin mass production to fill the orders and build an inventory for the additional orders that kept coming in every day after the show.

The journey is never-ending. There's always gonna be growth, improvement, adversity; you just gotta take it all in and do what's right, continue to grow, continue to live in the moment.

—ANTONIO BROWN

I first went to the bank to take out a loan, but the only way they would loan me the money was if I put my home up as collateral. It was a huge risk for not just me but also my family, but I knew that risk is one of the things both entrepreneurs and warriors have to embrace. I was able to use that loan to help fill those first orders, but as sales increased, I needed more help not only producing enough inventory but also building a team to help grow the business.

Eventually, I started to pitch my ideas to various investors and venture capital investment firms. I spoke with many venture capital firms, but one of my childhood mentors and his son introduced me to a small venture capital investment firm run by another father and son team. They assured me that when things got tough, and they always do, they would be there for me. Their commitment and the support of the investors made all the difference in our growth and success.

A warrior is only as strong as their team and those who support them. In a battle, as in business, you rarely can be successful on your own. As our firefighting business grew, we wanted to find ways to expand our portfolio of products to those whom the firefighters protect—the general public. We expanded our offerings to other safety products such as exit signs that never need batteries, lightbulbs, or electricity. We also made products that went into stairwells so that if the power failed, the glow in the stairwells would light the way out of the building. We created a new brand called LumAware® for these products.

LumAware® Team, Cincinnati, Ohio

The company continues to grow to this day as we now have three of the nation's four largest retailers using our products and even have our products now distributed by some of the nation's largest distributors like The Home Depot and HD Supply. We employ over a dozen people and have averaged close to ten million dollars in revenue over the last few years. We have about 100,000 firefighters in over twenty-five countries using our products. As the coronavirus started to spread, we pivoted to make protective barriers and products resulting not only in more lives saved but also in a drastically expanded source of revenue.

Author Zachary Green Preparing to Testify in front of the
US House of Representatives Small Business Committee, US
Capital, Washington, DC

I've received many awards and accolades for this entrepreneurial journey, ranging from the Entrepreneur of the Year award from the governor of Ohio to the President of the United States' E-Award for Exporting. I was even asked to testify in front of the US House of Representatives Small

Business Committee and was invited to the White House to share my experiences as an entrepreneur. President Obama selected me as one of ten entrepreneurs to represent the United States at the Global Entrepreneurs Conference.

Author Zachary Green, West Wing, The White House, Washington DC

Author Zachary Green, West Wing, The White House, Washington DC

However, the greatest accolade was being selected to represent the ten of clubs in the Frontline Leaders deck of cards based off of the deck of cards used in the Iraq War to identify the high-value Iraqi criminals. The Frontline Leaders cards were produced by the US Playing Card Company and developed by Capt. Marjorie Eastman who helped distribute the original deck of cards in Iraq. Her goal was to find fifty-two veteran-owned companies and honor them with their own card. LumAware was featured with other iconic veteran-founded companies such as Grunt Style Apparel, Black Rifle Coffee, Wounded Warrior Foundation, and Team RWB, to name a few. All these other warriors used what they learned in the military to battle their way through the challenges of being an entrepreneur.

Frontline Leaders Founder, Marjorie Eastman (left); US Playing Cards President, Michael Slaughter (center); LumAware® Founder, Zachary Green (right), Nashville, TN

Post- 9/11 Deck of 52, Frontline Leaders, 10 of Clubs, LumAware®

As humans, we have an innate desire to protect ourselves by taking the safe route. We are inclined to continue doing what we have done for ages. But in that process, we lose our inner warrior.

During my journey, I had to make many difficult and risky moves to keep the business afloat. The easy thing is to give up, the hard thing is to stick it out and make a start-up company work. It is in that adversity, hard work, and peril that the warrior is strengthened.

There were times that were so hard and scary. I considered quitting and filing for bankruptcy several times, but my warrior spirit kept me from giving in and quitting.

When you feel like stopping, remember: A warrior never gives up!

"Most of the important things in the world have been accomplished by people who have kept on trying when there seemed to be no hope at all."

—DALE CARNEGIE

CHAPTER 3

THE WARRIOR SPIRIT

———

Is any man afraid of change? What can take place without change? What then is more pleasing or more suitable to the universal nature? And can you take a hot bath unless the wood for the fire undergoes a change? And can you be nourished unless the food undergoes a change? And can anything else that is useful be accomplished without change? Do you not see then that for yourself also to change is just the same, and equally necessary for the universal nature?

—MARCUS AURELIUS

According to the Merriam Webster dictionary, one of the definitions of a warrior is a person engaged or experienced in warfare *broadly*: a person engaged in some struggle or conflict. I believe most of us would state the importance of warriors and how conflict has been essential over the years in shaping the world. That conflict and adversity is what both shapes and guides the change that the aforementioned quote from Marcus Aurelius speaks about. Personal and professional growth is very difficult if you don't stress and challenge yourself. Throughout history, warriors and conflict are included in almost every era. However, conflict doesn't have to be limited to war. Conflict comes in many forms ranging from physical battles to internal growth. Conflict could be physically fighting an enemy, or it could also be growing and learning from adversity. It is in that conflict that a warrior spirit shines.

"Out of every one hundred men, ten should not even be there, eighty are just targets, nine are real fighters, and we are lucky to have them, for they make the battle. Ah, but the one, the one is a warrior, and he will bring the others back."

—HERACLITUS, GREEK PHILOSOPHER

This quote was from thousands of years ago. It is just as true then as it is today. Warriors, like entrepreneurs, are a rare breed. Even though warriors don't sell innovative products on the battlefield and entrepreneurs don't fight with guns and swords, they still have quite a bit in common. It is what drives both the warrior and the entrepreneur that has so much in common. Through the following pages of this book, you will learn from their stories highlighting the intangible common traits. Regardless of if you are an entrepreneur, soldier, manager, or student, any of us can learn from these traits and the stories that are examples.

Warriors have been found throughout history, and we will not only explore the warriors of the past but also current warriors in modern times. We will be focusing on the intangibles that shape the warrior spirits found both in the military and in the warriors of industry that start and run their own businesses. Those intangible traits that make up the warrior spirit will be highlighted in future chapters. Those chapter traits are:

Teamwork
Purpose
Confidence
Adaptability
Tenacity
Grit
Sacrifice
Morals
Purpose
Serenity

SAMURAI

Being a warrior means battling anything and everything that might be an obstacle and fighting like no one before. From the Egyptian Pharaohs who presented themselves in war carriages smashing and throwing spears at enemies, to the European mounted knights, to the samurai in Japan, our history is filled with precedents that proudly display the fighting spirit.

Let's begin by talking about the samurai and their warrior spirit. Even if we aren't familiar with the real samurai, we have been introduced to them through pop culture. The samurai, also known as bushi, were a group of warriors that came into noticeable existence back in the tenth century CE in Japan. They performed military service until the tenth century and were trained warriors who could use the bow as well as the sword. They were popular and essential to Japan's medieval armies.

The interesting thing to note about them is that they were multi-skilled. When they encountered a hurdle, instead of using that hurdle as an excuse to fail they used their training and cultural influences to conquer these hurdles. The samurai were known for having a very diverse background. Not only were they highly skilled swordsmen, but they also studied poetry, were skilled in the art of the tea ceremony, calligraphy, painting, and rock gardens. This gave them an unmatched ability to improvise, overcome, and adapt to virtually any scenario both on and off the battlefield. Just like a samurai has to be prepared for any scenario and use many different weapons, so must an entrepreneur be skilled in many different tools to accomplish their entrepreneurial mission.

They accepted the adversity and became the epitome of chivalry and honor in Japan. Their warrior spirit made them into significant moral leaders and advisors in their society. From being servants of the imperial court and not just another class of warriors, they became enduring examples of courage and resilience because of their commitment to a higher purpose, in this case the god-like emperor.

Times changed, and peace prevailed. Military skills were no longer a need, so the samurai diversified. They became bureaucrats, artists, teachers, and entrepreneurs. It is simple: if you are a true warrior and you take change as a challenge instead of a mind-boggling problem, you will make it through. The samurai, one of the most famous warrior classes in the history of humanity, had these attributes. The samurai were a living example of the warrior trait of putting a higher cause and calling above themselves.

SPARTANS

Where the samurais were fighting in the East, the Spartans were battling the enemies of ancient Greece. Your first recollection of the Spartans may be heavily influenced by pop culture and particularly a movie named 300 that came out in 2006. Although the movie had an almost cliche superhero movie cinematography and special effects, it was surprisingly accurate. The Spartans were fearless, bold, and resolute in their ways, and they were phenomenal warriors. For the Spartans, being a warrior wasn't just about their skills on the battlefield; it was a way of life that warriors and others still admired today. As a matter of fact, 334 high schools, colleges, and professional sport teams count the Spartans as their mascot, including my high school alma mater, Roger Bacon.

Roger Bacon High School, Spartan Mascot

From birth, Spartans faced challenges they were taught to overcome. Skills like fighting, physical fitness, and practices like obeying orders were taught to them at an age where, in comparison, today's children are playing with gaming consoles. The training went as far as staged battles set up for children, starting around the age of seven. The training went on until these individuals were twenty-nine.

Another huge challenge was that Spartan children did not live with their families. Instead, they inhabited large living quarters with other children. Being away from parents is incredibly tough, but it also makes a child fiercely independent. These may sound like harsh measures today, but this adversity helped them grow and thrive on the battlefield. From early childhood, Spartans were given challenge after challenge that would be considered sadistic and cruel by today's standards. The physical and mental toll was tremendous but through that adversity they grew. This growth is what contributed to their legendary status even today, millenniums later. The harsh challenges they faced during those formative years prepared them for the future battles they would fight.

The most well-known battle of the Spartans occurred at a mountain pass named Thermopylae. In that battle, a mere 300 Spartans, led by King Leonidas, defended themselves despite being ridiculously outnumbered.

How did they achieve all of this? How did 300 men defend themselves in front of a huge and seemingly undefeatable army? It was through strategy and the warrior spirit of never giving up even though the 300 were going up against between 100,000 and 150,000 men that King Xerxes had. The 300 Spartans found a narrow mountain pass that would allow them to funnel the Persians into a narrow road so that they would lose their advantage of greatly outnumbering the Spartans. Just like a small entrepreneurial business that competes against a large corporation, you can be victorious if you have a strong team executing a well-developed strategy.

The common theme amongst all warriors and those who possess the warrior spirit is **grit**. Never giving up, embracing adversity, and using challenges as opportunities for growth are all areas that separate the warrior from the common man. Throughout history, warriors have adapted according to the situation presented to them. They rarely gave up because things got rough or didn't unfold based on the original plan. They adapted, improvised, overcame, and prevailed. This is why it's so crucial for an entrepreneur to adopt the mindset of a warrior. When you start with a business idea, you need to possess grit as the path to success is rarely easy. Mission accomplishment has to take priority over personal comfort. There is a solution to EVERY problem an entrepreneur faces, but unless you adopt the warrior spirit, many may not want to do what is necessary to solve those problems. You need to draw from varying experiences of your life, and most importantly, you must have that fighting warrior spirit within you. Let the warriors in this book inspire you to prevail and succeed no matter what challenges you encounter.

It is unlikely that you'll find mediocre, safe players in history books. Being a warrior isn't easy. It is never a comfortable path to take. However, the adversities and challenges that we think might derail us are what make us stronger and more successful. When we talk about being a warrior, keep in mind it has little to do with physicality and everything to do with grit. For an entrepreneur, it is essential to possess the mental and emotional fortitude exemplified by the warriors in this book.

"Whatever you are physically...male or female, strong or weak, ill or healthy—all those things matter less than what your heart contains. If you have the soul of a warrior, you are a warrior. All those other things, they are the glass that contains the lamp, but you are the light inside."

—CASSANDRA CLARE, CLOCKWORK ANGEL

Warriors make up a significant part of world history. Where the samurai and Spartans were warriors of territorial and ethnic wars, it is the common theme that connects them with other warriors: embracing and learning from adversity.

ENTREPRENEURS

If we consider this from an entrepreneur's perspective, it could mean two things. A safe thinker would probably convince themselves that the risk of putting all their money into something wasn't a safe option. This is the reason few leave the safety of their nine-to-five jobs to take the challenging path of entrepreneurship. However, the warrior spirit would tell you that you must embrace the risk and adversity of the entrepreneurial journey in order to sustain success. As the old saying goes, no risk equals no reward. Although the easy path is the path most people follow, an entrepreneur and someone who wants to make a remarkable difference will look at risk as a motivator, not a barrier. Warriors know that a great challenge brings great rewards.

The case can be similar for entrepreneurs. They, too, use all their life experiences as well as their skills to change things not just for themselves, but for people around them. Look at Thomas Edison, for example. For years, he has been extolled as one of the most successful inventors from the United States. His inventions include devices in electric power generation, mass communication, motion pictures, and even sound recording. Edison used his creativity to form General Electric, a business that continues to be one of the biggest corporations in the world.

He is a classic example of the warrior spirit, taking challenges head on and also creating things that don't just benefit him, but also help the people around him. That's exactly what Thomas Edison did; he identified a problem—the world could do much better with a little more light—and hence he gave birth to General Electric and illuminated the world through his discovery. Most importantly, Edison never looked at failure as the end. He knew that failure and adversity are part of the entrepreneurial journey. In fact, a reporter once asked Edison, "How did it feel to fail 1,000 times?" Edison stated, "I didn't fail 1,000 times. The light bulb was an invention with 1,000 steps." Edison went on to say, "Great success is built on failure, frustration, even catastrophe."

Thomas Edison recognized the same thing that warriors recognize: adversity, failure, and resistance are all key to the growth needed for success. When change and challenge come to us, our usual response is to avoid and fear it. History endorses it, and religions validate it. If you look around yourself, you will find many examples of people who behave like warriors, think like warriors, and lead very successful lives because of it.

Once you become a true warrior with your heart, mind, soul, and spirit, you will find yourself helping others too. Being a warrior is all about making an impact and imparting your knowledge and wisdom to other entrepreneurs, especially those starting their entrepreneurial journey.

Follow the warrior way and embrace resistance and adversity and opportunities for growth. Find the lesson in your challenges and embrace them as lessons. Use courage to face your challenges head on, look at them as lessons, and you too will become a warrior.

CHAPTER 4

THE SCIENCE OF ADVERSITY

———

"Every difficulty in life presents us with an opportunity to turn inward and to invoke our own submerged inner resources. The trials we endure can and should introduce us to our strengths... Dig deeply. You possess strengths you might not realize you have. Find the right one. Use it."

—EPICTETUS

The world around us has changed radically. From the ancient times of historical warriors who fought brutal conflicts to the current age of convenience, the change is dramatic and total. It isn't just drastic in terms of the outcomes and results, but also the process. In fact, it is the difference in process that has transformed strong individuals into relaxed ones. According to John Warner in his review of *The Coddling of the American Mind: How Good Intentions and Bad Ideas Are Setting Up a Generation for Failure* by Jonathan Haidt and Greg Lukianoff, "The authors argue that children suffer under a culture of 'safetyism' where parents endeavor to protect their offspring from harm, and in doing so, prevent them from developing the necessary skills of resilience. They believe this plays a factor in some of the campus speech disputes as students are acculturated to fearing anything that may prove challenging and react accordingly."

As an example, many schools and universities have "safe spaces," a place where they can retreat to so they don't have to engage in counterpoints or views opposing theirs. Another example is in an effort to make sure everyone feels like a winner; we move from recognizing only the winners but rather we give trophies, rewards, and medals to everyone solely for participating. Over the years, we have slowly eliminated adversity and competition from our children's experiences. We are so focused on making everyone feel good that we are robbing them of the opportunity to learn from adversity and challenges. When we look at it from a broader perspective, we will quickly realize these safe spaces and participation trophies hinder the growth of children in the longer run.

In particular, young adults aren't taught to thrive, compete, and be the best; they are encouraged to place happiness and comfort above all else. Adversity and challenges build character. Imagine a baby learning to walk the first time. If we never gave them the opportunity to fall down, they would never learn how to walk. If you carried them everywhere rather than encouraging them to crawl and eventually walk to you, you would never let them grow. Mediocrity and making everyone a winner during the school years combined with safe spaces and eliminating debate with differing views in college may make our students feel good, but are we really helping them? Is their life really better if we eliminate challenges and adversity but we fail to prepare a child for the unavoidable challenges later in adulthood? Imagine their first job out of college and they encounter a difficult boss and challenging working environment. For many of the aforementioned students, this could be the first time in their life they have really been challenged. That stress and lack of preparation for this environment could be debilitating.

The decision is up to us now. Do we continue to coddle our upcoming generation, or do we give them the opportunity to learn from challenges that they need to grow and become better versions of themselves? In the real world, when these people with lots of participation trophies aren't praised for merely existing, or they receive criticism about their work, they often break down. They can't tolerate the pressure and are not equipped to deal with it.

Fortunately, it isn't because they *can't* handle it; it is only because their upbringing and socialization kept them safe. They have never really been allowed to think out of the box and then work through things like a warrior. Imagine if the great Muhammad Ali took this approach to training. What if he took the easy path to training and just stopped when things got tough or when he was being pushed too hard by his coaches and trainers? He knew his growth was in the suffering, and he endured during training.

"I hated every minute of training, but I said, 'Don't quit. Suffer now and live the rest of your life as a champion.'"

—MUHAMMAD ALI

Student athletes tend to experience more adversity and challenges in high school and college than their non-athlete peers. For example, a study published in the Journal of Leadership & Organizational Studies showed that former high school and college athletes tend to have higher-status careers than non-athletes. The study found that employers assume former athletes to exhibit significantly more leadership, self-confidence, and self-respect than those outside of sports. In addition to the aforementioned study a Gallup-Purdue study found higher levels of engagement and well-being in the workforce after college. It could be surmised that the challenging training and competition of college athletes better prepare student athletes for the hardships and challenges encountered in post-college life.

Many well-respected professions require individuals strong, tough, and ready to face adversities. The military comes to mind, as one of the central themes in military training is to push recruits to their limit to show them that they are capable of more than what their civilian counterparts can handle. Military training is rigorous and difficult, but it is in that difficulty that the military shapes a civilian into a warrior that can accomplish anything they put their mind to. Again, this is where we can emphasize how vital the warrior spirit is for people who want to grow. For any businessperson, it is crucial to develop this warrior spirit. If you're attracted to challenges and growth, success is attracted to you.

Researchers and scientists have worked on this particular idea for some time. Biology, through our nervous systems, explains how and why we react to challenges the way we do, and why we sometimes don't respond to challenges the way an ideal warrior should.

Let's dive a little bit into biology and see exactly how our nervous system works and is connected to the way we react to adversities that come our way.

There are times in a human being's life where an approaching deadline, a forthcoming event, or even perhaps a man-eating shark comes their way. Faced with such a situation, our bodies tend to trigger a physical stress response. This stress response is what prepares us to either stay and fight or take flight. Fight or flight is the instinct that makes us decide if we want to run away from the challenge or, like a warrior, stand there and fight it. This response is mainly driven by our sympathetic nervous system. The sympathetic system makes up part of our autonomic nervous system. It regulates essential bodily functions like pupil dilation, heart rate, body temperature, blood pressure, digestion, and sweating.

Distinct types of nerve cells, called neurons, control these different physical reactions by directing the action of skeletal muscle, cardiac muscle, and gland secretion. The system allows animals to make quick internal adjustments and react without having to think about it.

—AMERICAN JOURNAL OF PHARMACEUTICAL EDUCATION

I witnessed a perfect example of the sympathetic nervous system in action in May of 2021 just a few steps from our home in Hilton Head Island, SC. A good friend and business associate joined me and a few friends for a walk on the beach. It was low tide and the sandbar about a quarter mile away was exposed. This created a natural barrier during the low tide that trapped fish. This beach was just off the Port Royal Sound, which is known as a common ground for tiger, hammerheads, and great white sharks. According to DNR marine biologist Bryan Frazer, "The sound might have the largest concentration of tiger sharks of any non-ocean area in the state or East Coast." My friend, being not only a former Marine but also a member of the elite Force Reconnaissance community, decided it would be "cool" if he could swim out to the sandbar and back. Before his wife and I could say anything, he dove into the water and started to swim to the distant sandbar. A few minutes later, we noticed commotion in the water and saw other people on the beach running to the water. All we heard was, "Your friend is in trouble." As we started to walk toward where he was coming out of the water, his face was ashen white, his eyes were wide open, and his breathing was elevated. He sat on the beach and shared that he had just been attacked by a shark. He stated he first felt the shark rub next to his foot, and he instantly knew that the sandpaper-like texture could only mean one thing: shark. He said he immediately switched to survival mode as memories of his combat experiences in Iraq came to mind. He said he didn't think; he just reacted. He recalled he could feel a rush of both fear and adrenaline take over his entire body. As the shark turned to make another pass at him, he kicked it in the head. The shark eventually swam away but it was his sympathetic nervous system that prepared him for the life-threatening encounter. A warrior's courage to meet challenges head on and use all the tools they both consciously and subconsciously possess is what makes them prevail in situations that could literally destroy the common man.

The sympathetic nervous system decides the immediate and involuntary reaction to stressful or possibly dangerous situations. Hormones begin to boost the alertness of the body along with pumping up the heart rate and transferring extra blood into the muscles. Other actions include the quickening of breathing, fresh oxygen being delivered to the brain, and infused glucose shot into the bloodstream for that adrenaline rush you may feel.

The severity and speed of all these responses is so quick it becomes close to impossible for a human being to realize it's happening, let alone control it. For example, you might be on your way to begin a business, and you lose your primary investor. Your first response isn't one you can control. By the time you get control over yourself, you would have given your first response already.

The human body has a natural way of balancing the stress created from a sympathetic nervous response. This is because once the sympathetic nervous system has responded to danger by stressing your body, it doesn't undo the stress on its own. Something needs to happen to bring your body back in balance. The body's natural way of returning yourself to a neutral state after a sympathetic response is the result of the parasympathetic nervous system. It calms our body down and begins to undo everything the sympathetic nervous system did. The first sympathetic system works toward countering and taking care of the fight or flight response while the second system encourages the body to rest and digest. Our bodily functions, like stable blood pressure, breathing rate, heart rate, and even hormone flow, tend to return to normal levels as our body settles into homeostasis (an equilibrium state).

Science and biology explain our behavior and responses in regard to the sympathetic and parasympathetic nervous system that work together to maintain this baseline and normal body function. By understanding these processes, you can learn to train your mind to allow it to handle stressful and challenging situations when necessary because the body will naturally "heal itself" after the event has passed. Understanding and controlling the fight or flight concept is something you can learn. If you tend to avoid problems and always run from a challenge, you never give your body a chance to work in the way it was intended. Take for instance a young student being picked on by the playground bully.

Every day the bully threatens and even may hit him in order to get his lunch money. The student has two choices: to run away every time he sees the bully or to stand up to him. The warrior spirit in the student could take self-defense classes like karate or mixed martial arts. He will use the training and adversity he learns in the rigorous classes to train and grow. His confidence will build, but most importantly, he will learn the science of hand-to-hand combat. It won't be easy as he moves through the ranks of the classes and participates in the difficult drills, but he will build confidence and courage knowing he has not only not quit but he also sees the weekly improvements.

Utilizing the fight system doesn't necessarily mean you are going to physically fight the threat; it means courage and fortitude will allow you to confront the obstacle head on and not run away from it. When the student encounters the bully, he doesn't even need to fight him. He can stand up to him with the confidence and courage of a warrior. His confidence and attitude in his stance and his newfound training that he knows is superior to the bully lets him know he can win the conflict without even having to throw a punch. It is because he used the adversity of his training to grow and learn that enabled him to switch from a flight situation to a fight situation because he looked at the obstacle and learned how to defeat it.

There is no difference in this concept for an entrepreneur. Starting a company is ridiculously difficult. Very few businesses can even survive after the first year. As a matter of fact, according to the Small Business Administration, in 2019, the failure rate of start-ups was around 90 percent. Research concludes 21.5 percent of start-ups fail in the first year, 30 percent of the remaining businesses fail in the second year, 50 percent of the remaining businesses fail in the fifth year, and 70 percent of the remaining businesses fail in their tenth year. The common thread among most of the start-ups that failed is that the founders decided to give up. **Giving up is easy; it is prevailing through the challenges and adversity that is so difficult.** The converse is also true in that the businesses that succeeded used the adversity as an opportunity to learn from their past mistakes and grow.

It is up to you how you want to deal with the situations that come your way. Do you want to defeat them by choosing to fight? Or do you want to avoid them by choosing to flee? It is safe to assume that if you pick "fight" as your response to stress, danger, and uncertainty, then you have the warrior spirit and will make a successful entrepreneur. But if you choose flight, you probably will have trouble making it through the adversities that come from starting and growing a business.

EARLY ADAPTORS

The fighters display courage and innovation. A common thread with entrepreneurs is their ability to try new things and innovate. They are always trying to find simple and elegant solutions to problems. They find ways to tackle any and every problem that comes their way. Simon Sinek, a motivational speaker, talks about innovation and how those who choose to fight, the people with a warrior spirit, approach diversity with a positive outlook:

"So it's this here, this little gap that you have to close, as Jeffrey Moore calls it, 'Crossing the Chasm'—because, you see, the early majority will not try something until someone else has tried it first. And these guys, the innovators, and the early adopters, they're comfortable making those gut decisions. They're more comfortable making those intuitive decisions that are driven by what they believe about the world and not just what product is available."

You will recall this is how I personally developed and grew my business idea that eventually became my start-up company. From my life experiences and the adversity I went through from different jobs to my time in the US Marine Corps, I learned to embrace adversity and challenges and to use them as learning opportunities.

Let me give an example. I started my company as the result of a very horrifying situation. I was a rookie firefighter and found myself lost and disoriented in a structure fire. The smoke had blocked out all natural light and the electricity was no longer functioning. It was so dark I couldn't even see my hand in front of my face. As luck would have it, my flashlight was out of batteries, and the ability to see was gone. I could only rely on my sense of touch, which was greatly diminished due to the bulky firefighting gear and thick fireproof gloves. I thought I was coming to the end of a hallway, knowing either the stairs or doorway would be at the end of the hallway and hopefully lead me to safety. However, there was no door or stairwell, only another wall. I was so disoriented it turned out I was actually in a large walk-in closet.

At this point I looked at my air regulator supply gauge and saw I was getting dangerously low on air. I had to find my way to fresh air soon or I could be in a critical situation. I remembered my training and followed the hose line in reverse, which eventually led me to the outside. Many people would quit and never subject themselves to a situation like this again. However, I felt the opposite, I looked at this as a challenge to overcome and an obstacle to conquer. I became obsessed with investigating other lighting technologies that could be used by firefighters to see in the dark, thereby reducing disorientation and increasing accountability. The challenge I encountered is that firefighters tend to be very set in their ways. There is a common saying: "Firefighters hate change but always complain about keeping things the way that they are." It was up to me to find the early adapters—the firefighters willing to try something different, the ones always looking for the next "thing." Once I identified these characteristics, I had to show them why this new technology was so important. Social media is a great tool to reach like-minded people. I spent hours writing about disorientation and lack of accountability in black-out conditions. I posted videos, wrote blogs, and even was interviewed by various podcasts and media outlets. I shared my story of being lost in a fire so my fellow firefighters would know why I was on this journey. Once I identified the early adaptors, I had them join me on this journey by making them part of my sales team. Eventually, I had over 300 early adopter firefighter sales reps that helped convince the other firefighters at their station or nearby departments why this technology was so important. Simon Senik summed up these processes by stating,

"People don't buy what you do; they buy why you do it. And if you talk about what you believe, you will attract those who believe what you believe. But why is it important to attract those who believe what you believe? Something called the law of diffusion of innovation, and if you don't know the law, you definitely know the terminology. The first 2.5 percent of our population are our innovators. The next 13.5 percent of our population are our early adopters. The next 34 percent are your early majority, your late majority, and your laggards. The only reason these people buy touch tone phones is because you can't buy rotary phones anymore."

This idea eventually turned into a portfolio of glow in the dark products now used by almost 100,000 firefighters in over twenty-five countries. Had I given up after becoming lost, I would have never had the opportunity to achieve the success my company has experienced over the last decade.

"That which does not kill us makes us stronger."

—FRIEDRICH NIETZSCHE

It isn't just biology concerned with our adversity and stress responses. There is considerable philosophical material on the same subject. German philosopher Friedrich Nietzsche emphasized how challenges only make us stronger and help us thrive to become the best versions of ourselves.

Nietzsche thought a little differently about how life and people function. He believed the mere pursuit of happiness is a dull waste of human life. For him, life was all about the idea of finding meaning. He offered the idea that people willing to go through a great deal of suffering would be better suited to achieve a goal they set than those who did not.

Nietzsche beloved that to be able to achieve success, people would need to look for meaning and fight for what they wanted to achieve. Nietzsche's philosophical ideas are also well supported by psychology. Victor Frankl said, "The key to good living is to find meaning, going so far as to suggest positive meanings for the suffering of his patients to help them carry on."

Being a warrior is a way for you to signal to others that you're unafraid, that difficulty won't break you, that adversity will only make you more confident. Embrace, learn, and grow from your adversity. Challenge yourself, and you will accomplish more than you can imagine.

"Believe in yourself, take on your challenges, dig deep within yourself to conquer fears. Never let anyone bring you down. You got to keep going."

—CHANTAL SUTHERLAND

CHAPTER 5

THE CONCEPT OF CRUCIBLES

———

"Strength does not come from winning. Your struggles develop your strengths. When you go through hardships and decide not to surrender, that is strength."

—ARNOLD SCHWARZENEGGER

We start this chapter with a quote by one of the strongest men in modern history. Not only was Arnold Schwarzenegger a movie star, entrepreneur, and governor, but he also played one of the great warriors of fantasy, Conan. As Arnold stated above, struggles show up for everyone, and these struggles can make or break us.

We have discussed the warrior spirit, followed by the adversity that supports it. Now, we must also consider how adversity prepares us for challenges, some of which end up being our crucibles. Everyone who wants to make a difference in their lives and the lives of others, be it warriors, leaders, or entrepreneurs, goes through a turning point at some time. This turning point is known as a crucible: an event that challenges the soul and tests your mettle.

At the crucible, the warrior either fails and chooses to quit, or digs deep and realizes a transformation has to happen. The crucible can occur in the early phases of a warrior's training as they shed their civilian ways. It can happen to a combat-hardened warrior who encounters something so horrible that they have a difficult time processing what they experienced. It can happen many years later when repressed memories and PTSD rear their ugly face. It can happen to an entrepreneur when they realize they can't make payroll. It can happen to anyone when the path forward is interrupted by a stressful event.

In the crucible there is a crisis of faith, a crisis of existence, a crisis of what you believed to be true up to this point in your life—a point like this is when a warrior is made. Typically, a crucible is the most pivotal point in a warrior's life, and it occurs when we realize everything we believe in and everything that has gotten us where we are now is not enough.

THE ABYSS

"And if you gaze for long into an abyss, the abyss gazes also into you."

—NIETZSCHE

There comes a time during that crucible where you reach your personal "rock bottom." It is different for everyone. For the warrior, it could be the point where they are almost overrun by the enemy and they are down to their last rounds of ammo. It could be the point for the entrepreneur when they run out of money and can't figure out how they are going to keep the company from falling into bankruptcy. At the bottom of that crucible, the bottom of that stressful event is where the abyss lies. It could represent failure, surrender, or just giving up. It is the place where self-pity and failure reside. The great philosopher Nietzsche says if you stare at (spend too much time near) the abyss, it will literally consume you. The abyss represents failure, surrender, and ultimately death. It is important for all warriors to recognize the abyss is there but you shouldn't spend too much time focusing and staring at it, as it will eventually pull you into it.

When you are at the darkest moments you find yourself in your crucible and realize that to make it to the next step in your life's mission, you have to disconnect from your past, shed your former self, and transform.

At that moment, you take a personal inventory and look at what got you here and how to move forward.

The abyss consumes mental and physical scars, self-doubt, fear, tangible possessions, and bad relationships. Although you try to put chaos in order, you realize that it is in the chaos that you grow, learn, and transform into a true warrior. As the old African proverb says, "Smooth seas do not make skillful sailors." To grow, adapt, and truly overcome, you need this critical moment in your life. It is the training that makes you a warrior.

The quote above by Nietzsche also depicts exhilaration through danger. We know a significant challenge is necessary for the new, more transformational being to materialize. The depth of the abyss and the size of the challenge define the scope for greatness, which Nietzsche values above all else. A thirst for danger and a desire to overcome it are necessary for success.

An entrepreneur has to follow the same transformational journey. Most of the time, an entrepreneur leaves the safety of a traditional job to embark on their entrepreneurial journey. They have to follow the warrior's way. When they meet their crucible and look into their abyss, they realize what is most important. That's when they find their "why."

Before we explore how and why these crucibles occur in an entrepreneur's life, we must understand the idea of the crucibles and how they prepare the warriors of today.

THE CRUCIBLE AND HELL WEEK

Let's discuss the US Marines first. Training in the Marines has always been incredibly tough. The Marines balance that toughness with lessons and exercises showing the importance of mission accomplishment, integrity, teamwork, pride, and a connection to our former Marine warriors who passed the guidon from generation to generation of Marines. However, since 1996, they have pushed their training a notch higher. This transformative change from civilian recruit to finally earning the title of US Marine is now the keystone of the long recruit training.

It is as if it is designed to break the recruits, mentally and physically. This test, done within the training, is one that spreads over fifty-four hours, including deprivation in terms of food, sleep, and rest as the recruits march over forty-five miles in a short few days. It tests them physically, mentally, as well as morally to make sure they are worthy of the sacred US Marine title.

During the test, teams are pitted against one another through catastrophic battle scenarios and several day and night events. Recruits don't sleep for several days and have very limited food rations to simulate the stresses of actual combat. The recruits work together to solve problems, overcome obstacles, and come out showing they have what it takes to be US Marines.

These hurdles and obstacles are meant to test both the mental toughness, decision-making skills, teamwork, and small-unit leadership, all in an environment of intense physical and mental stress. They include complicated, dangerous, and intense obstacles like combat assault courses, long marches, team-building warrior stations, leadership dilemmas, and critical decision making. The crucible, for Marine recruits, is a rite of passage that allows them to improve themselves, learn the value of having a warrior spirit, and prevail over any challenge that confronts them. The ones who fail this test fail to become Marines.

Like the Marines, Navy SEAL Training has its own crucible; however, it is even more intense and drawn out.

"Right then, I knew for certain: there was indeed no mercy in Hell Week. Everything we'd heard was true. You think you're tough, kid? Then you go right ahead and prove it to us."

—MARCUS LUTTRELL, SEAL

BUDS (SEAL) Hell Week is undoubtedly one of the hardest military training events in the world. Every SEAL has to pass it. It is five and a half days of brutal operational training with less than four hours of sleep. Less than 25 percent of those who start hell week make it. According to NAVYSEAL.COM:

Trainees are constantly in motion: running, swimming, paddling, carrying boats on their heads, doing log PT, sit-ups, push-ups, rolling in the sand, slogging through mud, paddling boats and doing surf passage. Being still can be just as challenging, when you're standing interminably in formation, soaking wet on the beach, or up to your waist in the water, with the cold ocean wind cutting through you. Mud covers uniforms, hands, faces—everything but the eyes. The sand chafes raw skin and the saltwater makes cuts burn. Students perform evolutions that require them to think, lead, make sound decisions, and functionally operate when they are extremely sleep-deprived, approaching hypothermia, and even hallucinating. While trainees get plenty to eat, some are so fatigued that they fall asleep in their food. Others fall asleep while paddling boats and have to be pulled out of the water by teammates. Teamwork and camaraderie are essential as trainees alternately help and encourage each other, to hang in there and not quit.

It is the goal of the instructors to push the SEAL candidates to their own abyss. The ones who can't escape the abyss or spend too much time feeling sorry for themselves become consumed by the abyss and ring the bell announcing to all that they have quit.

Basic Underwater Demolition/SEAL (BUD/S) Obstacle Course, Coronado, CA

If you look around you, most successful people have overcome extreme struggles and problems to be where they are. They have conquered their crucibles. So far, we have talked about organizations like the US Marines and the Navy SEALs using crucibles to determine who is strong enough to respectively wear the eagle, globe, and anchor or the SEAL Trident Special Warfare insignia.

However, let's look at examples that may be more familiar for those outside the military. It is something that can happen to each one of us—to test our limits in the face of adversity and to test who we are as human beings.

Crucibles in entrepreneurship endure similar turning points, mostly in terms of mental and psychological challenges. In situations like these, you are pushed harder than you think you can endure, and it prompts you to ask yourself, *Will this challenge swallow me, or will I conquer it like the warrior I am?*

Take my experience when I started my company, for example. There were several times early in my entrepreneurial journey where the company was severely short of money. As with many young start-ups, we were spending more than we were making causing us to become critically low on cash. I had a prescheduled trip to Hawaii with my family, and I decided for the first time in many years, I was going to completely relax, focus on my family and my mental health, and not check emails. I told my CFO not to contact me unless it was business critical. Sure enough, I received a call a few days into our vacation from my CFO. My hands started to tremor as I answered the phone. His stern and non-emotional voice cut through the phone as he explained he didn't think we would have enough money to pay the upcoming payroll. This is about the worst-case scenario any small business owner can face. It typically means it's the end. As I hung up, I fell to my knees and couldn't catch my breath. As my tears began to flow, I felt a severe pain in my chest and a weird tingling feeling shoot down my arm. I knew I was having a heart attack. Thankfully my wife is a doctor and quickly diagnosed me with having a panic attack. Her recommendation was to try and calm down. She suggested I walk on the beach and soak up the beauty and aloha spirit of Hawaii. I went outside and dove into the neon blue waters of the lagoon. As I emerged from the water, I could feel the stress start to dissipate, and I remember retreating to the shade of a palm tree as I prayed for strength, direction, and the wisdom to make it through this crisis.

Quitting is the easy choice; it is in success where the difficulty lies. I knew the simple path was to accept the failure and give up, but I remembered my training in the Marines; improvise, overcome, adapt, but never give up. Over the next few days, my leadership team and I looked at many different options, and we were able to secure a short term note to bridge the time between paying payroll and replacing that cash with new sales. This was one of the first times I came close to the abyss as an entrepreneur. I didn't stare into the abyss for too long. I recognized I was falling close to it, but I used my warrior spirit to fight and prevail, leaving it behind me.

There are plenty of other success stories about people who have overcome adversity by virtue of their fighting spirit. One such success story is that of Momofuku Ando. This is the man you can thank on nights when you're hungry and don't have time to cook, so resort to instant noodles and ramen. Yes, he invented instant noodles! The noodles are instant, but his journey and eventual success weren't all that quick.

Ando was from Japan, the land of samurai. Technically, he was born and spent a considerable amount of time in Taiwan, but back in 1910, Taiwan was under Japanese rule. Following in the footsteps of his family, he set up a company to sell Japanese-made knitted fabrics. The business flourished and also made it to Osaka, a financial hub, but soon after the Second World War commenced, he lost a significant amount of business. This was Ando's first struggle, which he overcame by improvising. He branched out into manufacturing rudimentary post-war housing and salt and also founded a school. This is what having a strong spirit does for an entrepreneur. The moment unavoidable and unforeseen circumstances hit, you come up with different ways to tackle them.

The war hampered Ando's financial and entrepreneurial success in multiple ways. He was arrested for the first time in the early war era, as he was accused of diverting military goods into the black market. Another arrest hit him after the war, under the criminal act of tax evasion. In both cases, he was set free soon after being proven innocent.

Ando's real and most significant crucible came in 1957 when a credit union he headed went utterly broke. Apart from one rental property in Osaka, Ando lost all of his wealth overnight. Just like that, everything was gone. Unfortunately, in cases like these, most people would either retire or become helpless, especially if they were in their late forties like he was. But Ando was cut from a different fabric. Being a true warrior, he was bent but not broken. He looked at all of it as an experience that would serve him well. He worked on an idea that came to him at a black market near Osaka's central train station in the post-war era, where food shortages were widespread.

He saw people standing in long queues for their turn to get a bowl of ramen. This is when it hit him that if there is one thing people will always buy, it is food. He also realized that with life becoming so fast paced, they would need food they could get faster. He considered how noodles are such a staple in Japan and used his insight into the needs of people to come up with his revolutionary plan.

> When you cast away all your greed
> and fixation in adversity, you can find
> unexpected strength.
>
> —MOMOFUKU ANDO

Ando built a small workshop behind his house and started developing the product. At this point, he was still struggling because he didn't know where his next meal would come from. He wasn't entirely out of his crucible yet, but he was carving a way out, one day at a time. The research continued, and for a year, Ando only got four hours of sleep a night with not a single day off. He was working hard to implement his plan and achieve what he aimed to do. Finally, it happened. His patience, perseverance, and experience paid off. This experiment in the name of instant ramen produced the world's first chicken ramen that eventually went on sale in the second half of 1958 and now is a global staple on virtually every grocery store shelf.

The warrior entrepreneur's journey is never linear; in 1957, Ando went bankrupt. This was the most significant financial hit of his life. Yet, in less than two years, he picked himself back up and created what is deemed essential today. Problems, obstacles, and hurdles kept challenging him, but like a true warrior, he slashed his sword of innovation across all of these problems, one after the other.

We know Ando's story now. We can prevail over our difficulties, walk out of that safe space, and embrace the adversity life throws our way. We need adversity. It prepares us for the fights to come. Everyone goes through their own set of crucibles, and everyone will face a turning point in their life. How one looks at that turning point, and what they make of it, is what defines them as a person. Don't be the one to sit back, give up, and take the safe route, because the world doesn't remember people who take the safe route, or give up. The world remembers warriors, and for warriors, crucibles are turning points for the better.

> "Show me someone who has done something worthwhile, and I'll show you someone who has overcome adversity."
>
> —LOU HOLTZ

CHAPTER 6

THE THREE PILLARS OF A SUCCESSFUL ENTREPRENEURIAL PLAN

———

"All men can see these tactics whereby I conquer, but what none can see is the strategy out of which victory is evolved."

—SUN TZU, THE ART OF WAR

Challenges are a part of life. You face them in your professional as well as personal life. The sooner we admit that challenges hone our skills, the better we become at making decisions and being successful. The ones who take these challenges head on make the most out of them. They defeat their opposition and are the ones we call warriors. This holds particularly true in the case of entrepreneurs. We talked earlier about how entrepreneurs need to be true warriors, but now let us talk about the roadmap to successfully starting and growing a business.

1 - THE ABILITY TO SOLVE A PROBLEM IN A UNIQUE AND ELEGANT WAY

Entrepreneurs with the spirit of a warrior will demonstrate several important qualities. The first pillar is the *ability to solve problems* in a unique and elegant way.

As a warrior, when you are presented with a matter of life and death, the way you choose to act defines you. Similarly, when you're an entrepreneur, you look for problems to solve. You cannot create a solution and then go around looking for a problem that it may or may not cater to. Pick up on the problem; that problem is then your challenge.

If we take a look at modern-day military training, we see a lot of problem-solving. It is no longer just about physical strength and abilities, but about being able to comprehend, and then battle challenges on the mental and emotional front.

Moreover, the increasing focus on developing teams and teamwork also stands as a testament to the idea that solving problems is a massive part of any form of military training. Solving problems together as a team only makes things more straightforward.

I feel that the diversity of a team is one of the best ways to solve a problem as it allows you to look at problems from different points of view. If everyone looked the same, had the same background, the same socioeconomic history, the team would only be able to look at a challenge one way. However, the more diversity a team has, the more different ways they can look at the same challenge and come up with different solutions.

War has evolved; warriors need to as well. We are our best selves when we embrace diversity rather than shun it.

As an entrepreneur, one of the ways I solved a problem in a unique and elegant way came from something all of us usually see on a daily basis: exit signs.

There are over 100 million exit signs in the USA. Those exit signs need light bulbs, electricity, batteries, and monthly testing. It not only costs money, but it is also bad for the environment as those batteries and light bulbs end up in landfills. Plus, substantial carbon dioxide is generated from the electricity needed to power all those exit signs.

However, the building and fire codes do not require exit signs to be electrified, they only require them to be visible for ninety minutes after the power goes out. We were able to use the same glow in the dark materials that we made for firefighters to make the EXIT signs glow bright and long enough to be visible for the code required ninety minutes.

These new exit signs solved the problems that electric exit signs presented *and* we were even granted a patent (US Pat. No. 10,127,843) to further protect this idea.

It was a simple idea that turned out to be much more challenging and difficult than I could have ever imagined. The building trades and facility maintenance fields are very resistant to change. We encountered many obstacles as we grew this technology from electric unions who thought we would take away electricians' jobs to competing electric exit sign companies who maligned our technology. Nevertheless, because of the warrior mindset, we embraced those challenges and learned from them. Our success was not only shown in our revenue growth and expansion of our team but also by three of our nation's four largest retailers now using our exit signs.

Author Zachary Green testifying in front of the US House of Representatives Small Business Committee, US Capital, Washington, DC

2 - UNFAIR COMPETITIVE ADVANTAGE

The second pillar is an *unfair competitive advantage*. If we look at Greek history and the Spartans, who were great warriors, a particular battle can help us understand the concept of unfair competitive advantage. This was the battle of Thermopylae.

In 480 BC, the Persian army was moving south through Greece in an attempt to invade. They had several successes along the way. To reach their destination, the Persians had to go through the coastal pass of Thermopylae. The Greek leader, Leonidas, led an army of about 7,000 Greeks, including 300 Spartans, and decided to prevent the Persians from invading and attacking. He knew they could never defeat the significantly larger army. He needed to come up with a competitive advantage. The Spartans had to come up with a way to make sure the fight was not fair. In battle and in business, rarely does the concept of fairness come into play.

Leonidas established his army at Thermopylae, hoping the narrow pass would funnel the Persian army toward their own force. This plan worked exceptionally well for the heavily outnumbered Greeks as it funneled the Persian army into a narrow pass that gave the Spartans a significant unfair advantage as they removed the advantage of mass of the Persian army by only allowing a few of them to fight a few at a time. For two consecutive days, the Persians were prevented from using their numerical strength to overwhelm them as the Spartans decimated the Persians with their long spears.

Had the Spartan warrior King Leonidas and his fellow Spartans not been betrayed by a deserter, they would have probably been victorious. Nevertheless, the Spartans fought to the last man and managed to contain most of the Persians for a considerable amount of time. This is a prime example of an unfair competitive advantage and how to use that advantage wisely.

When I look at my journey, I used an unfair competitive advantage as well. When I came up with the idea of providing firefighters with glow-in-the-dark lighting, I was a serving member of my neighborhood fire department. My unfair competitive advantage was the fact that I was one of them. Not only do the firefighters typically do the exit sign inspections, but about 100,000 are also familiar with the same glow in the dark technology that I helped develop. My unique idea was to have the firefighters act as ambassadors of this technology. When they found a building with a faulty or missing exit sign, they could bring up the fact that there was a new technology that didn't use batteries, light bulbs, or electricity. That technology not only met the fire code for exit signs *but* was also used and trusted by firefighters. Who better than a brother firefighter to sell to a firefighter? Who better to know the challenges firefighters encountered in the dark smoky hallways than a fellow firefighter? Who cares more for a firefighter than a member of the firefighting family?

Fire Lieutenant Zachary Green on assignment with the Detroit Fire Department, Detroit, MI

Using this unfair competitive advantage, I quickly built a network of about 300 firefighters who could act as my sales and distribution channel. It was my edge over any other larger corporation: no matter how many salespeople, budgets, and support they had, they didn't have the brotherhood, understanding of the challenges, and insight like a fellow firefighter. Like the Spartans, I had a better strategy than the large corporations trying to sell to firefighters.

I used strategy and creativity to battle giant corporations. I used that same strategy of an unfair advantage by partnering with the Cincinnati Association for the Blind and Visually Impaired to manufacture my exit signs. They were a nonprofit whose mission was to support individuals with visual impairments. We not only had the opportunity to support their noble mission, but we also were able to outsource the costly manufacturing machinery. We could share that with our customers, who then wanted to support us because we were helping the visually impaired. This partnership allowed us to focus on our why versus our what or how. Additionally, the federal government also recognizes the incredible work the National Industries of the Blind does and how it supports a disadvantaged part of our society. The Ability One program was created to mandate that blind industries would receive priority in government purchases. As a result of the program, we were able to contract with the US State Department of Overseas Builds Operation to have virtually every US embassy and consulate use our non-electric illuminating safety products. I feel the most touching part of this partnership is that we have people who can't see making products for those who can see but need to find their way out of the dark.

Know the enemy and know yourself; in a hundred battles you will never be in peril. When you are ignorant of the enemy but know yourself, your chances of winning or losing are equal. If ignorant both of your enemy and of yourself, you are certain in every battle to be in peril.

—SUN TZU, THE ART OF WAR

When I look at my own story, I realize that one major component that helped me overcome several challenges was keeping a close eye on all my competitors. Here, we must know our enemies and all their limitations. Once we know what they are lacking, we can capitalize on their shortcomings.

For example, bigger corporations lacked a personal touch as well as personal connections to make it in the firefighter market. I released this early on and when they focused on size and economic power, I focused on the personal touch. We put customer service before profits. We utilized social media to talk with our customers rather than advertising that talk to customers. We let them know that they were our fellow firefighters, and nothing was more important than their safety.

Author Zachary Green at the MN8® headquarters in Wyoming (Cincinnati) Ohio

3 - GREAT SALES AND MARKETING DISTRIBUTION

The third pillar is to have a *great sales and marketing distribution.* You can have the greatest product or solution in the world, but if no one knows about it or can't easily buy it, you will never be successful. Many entrepreneurs are so scared that their advantage will be lost if others find out about their idea that they spend more time protecting it than marketing it. They also spend significant money on patents; however, rarely do entrepreneurs realize the cost of the patent is not the patent itself but rather what the cost of defending the patent is. Just the process of applying for a patent can be thousands of dollars. It can be even more expensive if you have to overcome the examiner's objections (which almost always happens).

However, the real cost of the patent is the cost to defend it. Patent litigation can take years and cost millions of dollars, *and* you are not even guaranteed you will be successful in your litigation. Not all patents are useless for the entrepreneur. As we previously mentioned, we have an issued patent and have had several provisional patents; it is important to know how to strategically utilize them. Imagine if that same money and effort could be spent on marketing and distribution. It could even be spent on development to better improve your idea from your original patented idea. A great product without good marketing and distribution will never be successful.

Conversely, a mediocre product with great marketing and distribution can be wildly successful. Just think of the Pet Rock. It was just a rock, but it sold millions and made the entrepreneur, Gary Dahl (whose background was in advertising), millions. Think about bottled water. It's just water, a resource that is basically free, but marketed and distributed in a market. It made over eleven billion dollars in 2007 because it was distributed through Coca Cola, who already had relationships with the stores and advertising second to none.

You get the idea—marketing and distribution are key to any successful entrepreneurial venture. When you manage to have people marketing and selling your product or service well, you have succeeded in your venture.

In addition to the three aforementioned pillars is a simple yet powerful idea by one of today's great authors and speakers,

Simon Sinek. His TED Talk on his golden circle concept of What, How, and Why is a must to watch for anyone.

What—What are you offering? For example, what is your product or service, what are the features and benefits of it?

How—How will this help your readers? For example, what problems are you solving for your readers, what challenges are you helping them overcome?

Why—Why are you doing what you are doing? For example, why are you in business? Why did you develop your product or service?

My WHAT was using alternative lighting technology to light the way out of the dark.

My HOW was embedding rare earth elemental crystals in various products such as accessories for firefighters, materials for exit signs, and coatings for stairwells that glowed in the dark without the need for batteries, light bulbs, and electricity.

My WHY was to help my brother and sister firefighters, and ultimately help people find their way out of dark buildings at the same time, utilizing eco-friendly alternative lighting solutions and having zero waste to landfills. My WHY was also partnering with the National Industries of the Blind to help disadvantaged members of our society have meaningful and gainful employment.

Combining a unique solution that had an unfair advantage with great sales, marketing, and distribution, I created a company that has grown into a close to ten-million-dollar-a-year business from the trunk of my car.

CHAPTER 7

TEAMWORK

———

*"One piece of log creates a small fire, adequate to warm you up,
add just a few more pieces to blast an immense bonfire, large
enough to warm up your entire circle of friends; needless to say,
that individuality counts but teamwork dynamites."*

—JIN KWON

You will find many clichéd quotes about teamwork. However,
this is one cliché that I would, from experience, encourage!
It isn't just me, but many successful individuals throughout
world history have emphasized the importance of people
supporting each other and learning to work together to
achieve success.

Some of my favorites are:

Alone we can do so little, together we can do so much.
—Helen Keller

Together
Everyone
Achieves
More

Talent wins games, but teamwork and intelligence win championships. —Michael Jordan

Teamwork is the ability to work together toward a common vision. The ability to direct individual accomplishments toward organizational objectives. It is the fuel that allows common people to attain uncommon results.
—Andrew Carnegie

Individual commitment to a group effort—that is what makes a team work, a company work, a society work, a civilization work. —Vince Lombardi

People who work together and understand how to take a team forward are the real winners. When it comes to wars, a single warrior cannot take on the enemy. Similarly, when it comes to an enterprise, an individual entrepreneur cannot run the entire operations without help, support, and delegation.

Before I jump into giving you examples from world history about how teamwork was essential in driving success, I'll present my personal experience with collaboration.

The first time I understood the importance of teamwork was when I was training for the Marines, and we did virtually everything as a platoon. Eating, sleeping, exercising, learning, and even going to the bathroom was a team effort. We were virtually never allowed to do anything as an individual.

I distinctly remember the time I made a mistake during training, and my entire platoon was reprimanded but me. We were participating in drill (marching in formation) where the entire platoon moved as one entity. You could only hear one boot hit the ground, everyone would perfectly be aligned side to side and front to back as we executed the precision movements of marching as one. Drill is an essential part of our training. We did it many times a day for what would seem like hours on end. It was a critical training tool to learn instant obedience to orders and unit cohesion. One particular day, the drill instructor gave the command of "column right" and the entire platoon, as instructed, turned to the right, but I turned to the left. This caused the formation to fall apart as my fellow recruits bumped into me. As the drill instructor yelled and screamed at us, I braced myself for my punishment. However, the sadistic drill instructor came up with a punishment far worse than what I had anticipated.

The drill instructor yelled at me to stay where I was as he commanded the entire platoon to immediately report to the dreaded Pit. The Pit (sandbox) was an area behind the barracks marked off by long telephone poles posited in a square on the ground with the interior filled with sand. However, he told me to stand at attention just outside the pit so all the other recruits could clearly see the reason they were being punished. As my fellow recruits entered this nefarious plot of sand, they were immediately instructed to start doing push-ups. From there, they were told to do bend and thrusts followed by flutter kicks and then back to push-ups. There wasn't much room in the sandbox, so each exercise caused the recruits to kick and bump into each other. This ensured everyone was covered from head to toe in sand that stuck to their sweat-soaked clothes, making them feel like sandpaper. To add insult to injury as the recruits counted the number of repetitions, they had to say my name after each number. As I heard the moans and yells of "one Recruit Green, two Recruit Green, three Recruit Green," my embarrassment and remorse cut deep as my brother warriors were being punished because I had let the team down. My guilt was pure as I realized the drill instructor was not being sadistic, and he was instead teaching both me and my team the importance of teamwork.

The Pit, Marine Corps Recruit Depot, Parris Island, SC

"Unity is strength...when there is teamwork and collaboration, wonderful things can be achieved."

—MATTIE STEPANEK

It is a standard military practice to make teamwork an essential part of military training and also holds true when you start a business. It isn't just because you need support for things that you can do well; it is because there are things that you *can't* do well. Not everyone can be good at everything they attempt to do. The sooner this concept is embraced, the sooner success will be achieved. Division of labor, delegation, diversity of thought, and skills are critical aspects of successful teams.

Another incident that occurred while I was training for the Marines stays with me to date. I was paired with an individual who continued to fail almost all of the academic tests during recruit training. This other recruit wasn't stupid; he just thought differently. On the other hand, I was top in the platoon when it came to test scores. The drill instructors decided to have me mentor and train this other recruit. I was the top recruit in the platoon for this training evolution, while he was dead last. Regardless, I was pulled aside by the drill instructor and told if he didn't pass the make-up exams, I would also fail this section of training.

I had no choice but to help him out because my existence, reputation, and future were now suddenly conjoined with his. Had he failed, we both would have this negative mark in our permanent files, and there was a chance we would be recycled to the next platoon and have to take this section of training again. This is what teamwork is. When all of you stand for something, it isn't just yours anymore.

"It is literally true that you can succeed best and quickest by helping others to succeed."

—NAPOLEON HILL

I helped my teammate selflessly because I knew him failing would mean us failing, and failing isn't an option for Marines. This came full circle a few weeks later when we started to assemble and disassemble our M-16 rifles. This same recruit who was dead last in the academic evolution was the fastest at taking his M-16 apart and putting it back together. I, on the other hand, was one of the slowest. He took it upon himself to help me better learn my rifle and increase my disassembly and assembly times. I helped him and he helped me, that is the epitome of teamwork.

At the end of the day, it all comes down to how you support each other. If I keep talking about my experiences with the kind of training I had, the list of how important support is for warriors and entrepreneurs can go on and on. I learned valuable lessons I still hold close.

When I started working on how to use photoluminescent pigments to help firefighters reduce disorientation and increase accountability, it was a one-man show. I would handle the finances, sales, marketing, and everything else on my own. Those early days consisted of receiving orders, filling orders, making products, updating the accounting software, selling more products, packaging products, and the day usually ended up with me waiting in the local post office to ship everything. That worked well for me initially, but as time passed and my idea became popular, I realized there is only so much time in a day, and only so much one person could do. That day, I admitted to myself I needed help. I needed a team to keep things going smoothly.

I started to build a team, one person after the other, and noticed how I could accomplish more with a team than when I tried to do everything by myself. But there was a problem. They didn't care as much as I did, and their work often was not up to my high standards. Even though the company could work faster and more efficiently when I delegated to the team. However, one of my mentors pointed something out to me that I couldn't see. Even if someone can only do a job 70 percent of what you can do, if you hire two of them, they will actually do 40 percent more than you could alone. The team is important, but it is also important to let them feel empowered and valued. Even though you can do it better, let them. Hire great people, train them, and then get the hell out of their way.

GOOD FOLLOWERS MAKE BETTER LEADERS
Through all of this, I learned another important lesson from my journey, and through following others: To be a good leader, you have to be a good follower. There comes a time

when your leadership as an entrepreneur is not enough for you or your venture to grow. You will most certainly need someone to help you out.

When you are growing a business or fighting a war, there is little room for stubbornness and ego. It comes down to a choice between your team's success versus your stubbornness. Unfortunately for me, it took some time before I embraced this in my entrepreneurial journey.

At one point in my business, I realized I was hampering the growth of my venture. I was trying to run a multi-million-dollar-a-year venture like the early days when I did everything. The volume of decisions and responsibilities were overwhelming. It wasn't the big choices that were difficult; it was the vast number of small decisions that started to overwhelm me. Not only could I not keep up, but I realized I was the bottleneck preventing us from making it to the next level. I quickly realized the way to grow was actually to let go.

I hired a CEO and gave him the support to grow the company and for me to report to him. Entrepreneurs are great at starting companies, but can many times have difficulty running those companies once they take off. Being a visionary is a very different set of skills than being an integrator. Most successful CEOs help integrate the sales/marketing, operations, and finance divisions.

Our parents bring us into this world, love us, care for us, and consider us the most important people in their lives. However, at one point they have to let go and support them rather than do everything. Similarly, an entrepreneur works on an idea, thinks about it, brings it into existence, loves it, then lets it grow on its own. The best thing you can do is not to hold on to a particular position or support a designation you may have but to support your company that you have put so much into. The entrepreneur like the parent never leaves but rather falls into a visionary and supportive role.

Teamwork makes the dream work, but a vision becomes a nightmare when the leader has a big dream and a bad team.

—JOHN C. MAXWELL

WARRIOR TEAM

One of the most historical examples in terms of teamwork is undoubtedly the Apollo 11, 1969 Mission. This was the moon landing where Neil Armstrong, Buzz Aldrin, and Michael Collins stepped on the moon.

That one moment the entire world remembers, documents, and cherishes, when Neil Armstrong stepped on the moon, isn't just something that one official in NASA decided and made happen. It happened because teams of people were diligently working for years through research and trial to make it happen.

"I thought, well, when I step off it's just going to be a little step—a step from there down to there—but then I thought about all those 400,000 people who had given me the opportunity to make that step and thought it's going to be a big something for all those folks and, indeed for a lot of others that weren't even involved in the project, so it was kind of a simple correlation."

—*Apollo 11 Astronaut Neil Armstrong talking about his famous line, "That's one small step for man, one giant leap for mankind."*

As per NASA, a whopping 400,000 people were involved in making the moon landing a possibility and later, a reality. The teams included researchers, scientists, engineers, technicians, mathematicians, and many more groups that worked together to make history through this project. The moon landing is the ultimate example of how a well-connected team of well-picked individuals can change the course of history.

Another excellent example of teamwork and its benefits can be found in *The Iliad*. It's an epic, and one of the oldest texts of the world. It is attributed to the Greek poet Homer and came into its written form in the eighth century BC. *The Iliad* is basically about a breakdown in teamwork. In *The Iliad*, Agamemnon, the leader of the Greeks, offends his best warrior, Achilles. Agamemnon is forced by the gods to give up his slave girl. Since he has lost his slave girl, he selfishly steals Achilles' slave girl as his own to replace the one he was forced to give up. Agamemnon and Achilles start to argue and insult each other over this situation. The argument eventually sends Achilles into a rage. Trust erodes, the unity of the Greek army falls apart, and failure ensues.

In *The Iliad*, Agamemnon and Achilles' breakdown of team-work causes them to lose sight of the purpose that originally drew them together and motivated them to travel to Troy to defeat the Trojans. Instead, Achilles leaves his army and stops fighting as his fellow warriors remain on the field in a brutal fight. The breakdown of teamwork is so complete that Achilles encourages the Trojans, in hopes that his Greek army is so depleted and disparate they will finally recognize and appreciate his role on the team.

You can only do so much alone when it comes to running a business. No matter how much you would like to think you can work without a team, after a point, you just can't.

Let me bring back the Spartans once again. The Spartans carried their shields on the left side of their body, which allowed them to cover the blind spot of the warrior fighting next to them. This is a perfect example of teamwork during a complicated situation like that of a war.

An entrepreneur operates the same way. They have to make sure there is a team that isn't just working together but is also determined to cover for each other as well. Support is essential when it comes to working anything out in our favor. When I say support, I don't just mean support to run the business or win a battle. This support is also emotional and psychological. For both warriors and entrepreneurs, stress is a frequent visitor. Sometimes, this visitor stays for too long, and that leads to disastrous results personally and profes-sionally. That isn't something anyone wants to deal with—or at least, not alone or without a support system. We will get more into how we can support other warriors in the following paragraphs.

> "Teamwork is the ability to work together toward a common vision. The ability to direct individual accomplishments toward organizational objectives. It is the fuel that allows common people to attain uncommon results."
>
> —ANDREW CARNEGIE

SUPPORT FOR WARRIORS

We are all human beings who get affected by our surroundings and the people around us. No matter how strong you are, stress can be as bad as a slow poison for us and our health. A plethora of research has been done on how stress affects our physical and mental health.

About one-third of the research participants interviewed by Everyday Health confessed to seeing a medical professional for stress-related concerns. Now, even though one-third sounds like a ridiculously large percentage, keep in mind these are only the people who sought help. If we add the number of people who don't seek help, it will most certainly top 50 percent.

People always need other people to lift them and support them to make things happen. Having supportive individuals around you can keep stress at bay as well. This is how human nature works. Human beings are inherently social beings. They need to interact to be able to function correctly, especially in terms of mental health concerns. Since our reference point is warriors, let us look at how vital this emotional and psychological support is for them.

First, we need to understand that warriors, military personnel, and fighters experience a lot of traumatic incidents directly. Most of these individuals tend to store it in their minds and memories and then are troubled forever. Amid this trouble, what they need is support. Times can get dark and difficult for them as they battle through and witness blood, death, pain, and misery.

One particular study has talked extensively about the effects of trauma on men and women in the military not just on the battlefield, but also off it:

> "Descriptive analyses indicated that from 22 percent to 40 percent of military men and women experienced high levels of stress in their work or family and personal relationships. Overall, both military men and women were nearly twice as likely to report feeling high levels of stress in their military work (39 percent) than in their family life (22 percent)."

This kind of stress, even though rather prevalent in military departments, isn't just limited to fighters. Workplaces, especially if you are running them, tend to have similar pressures that draw you into making wrong decisions and playing with your health.

For situations like those, it is essential to have support and a team that stands with you. That team will also ensure you to take over in case of your absence. There can't be enough emphasis on the fact that networks are essential to sustain a business, primarily because of how high stress levels in workplaces are today.

As per Wrike's United States stress statistics from the year 2019, only a meager 6 percent of workers were reported as not being stressed. This means 94 percent of the working population today is stressed, out of which 23 percent have high stress levels, and another 6 percent have unreasonably high stress levels. It is almost as if working in a stressful environment is slowly becoming the rule instead of an exception. Hence, the need for support groups becomes more prominent. For example, organizations like Entrepreneur's Organization, Vistage, and YPO are all great support groups for entrepreneurs.

Support provided by friends, family, and co-workers reduces the negative effects of stressful situations on physical and emotional well-being (Schaefer et al., 1981).

There is no denying the fact that teamwork and support are integral parts of becoming successful and retaining that success. Entrepreneurs don't just need logistical support during office hours. They also need trustworthy assistance that makes sure their physical and mental health remain stable. This is why physical fitness, adequate sleep, hobbies, and mindfulness are so important to both the warrior and the entrepreneur. This support will make you flourish as a businessperson or a warrior and also help you be mentally sound, even in times of trouble.

"Individual commitment to a group effort— that is what makes a team work, a company work, a society work, a civilization work."

—VINCE LOMBARDI

CHAPTER 8

PURPOSE

"Purpose-led brands are more successful in acquiring and retaining customers. This may make intuitive sense, but it is also backed up by behavioral science: People buy things that make them feel good about themselves. And people do business with those they trust."

—ERNST & YOUNG

In this book, we have talked about how warriors and entrepreneurs are similar and how their journeys mirror each other. We have also discussed various attributes that an entrepreneur has in common with warriors, and what makes them the powerful force that they become. Now, we must talk about the varying disciplines that entrepreneurs and warriors need to possess.

Our first discipline is purpose—that driving force within you that gives you solid reasons to go ahead with your actions and thoughts. Everything, in fact, every successful venture in the world, had a purpose behind it. You don't wake up one day and decide to do something just because you feel like it. Your experiences lead you to develop a purpose.

This purpose becomes the ultimate motivation for us to achieve success and to make the difference we wish to see in our world. I say "our world" instead of the world because we have all created surroundings. In this regard, our world is what is close to us. It has problems that are ours and need a problem solver who can relate to all these concerns.

For instance, most people who enlist in armed forces and as first responders have the purpose of serving their country. They aim to protect their neighbors, their sovereignty, and their homeland. This is a meaningful purpose because the journey they undertake after they decide to put their intention into action isn't easy at all. The rigors of training, the life and death situations, and the mental, physical, emotional, and spiritual exhaustion are only for those who possess significant intestinal fortitude and the desire to put others before self. Interestingly enough, the same aspects come into play when a businessperson or entrepreneur decides to act on the purpose they feel strongly about.

These individuals build their businesses and a considerable chunk of their lives around a purpose that drives them. Many books, quotes, and TED Talks will tell you all about motivation and how you can achieve it in a few steps. But the reality is that for most people, motivation comes not from books or ten-minute videos, but their personal experiences.

Without a purpose rooted in experience, most things are just robotic behaviors. As warriors, we need a purpose to center our world and business around.

To thine own self be true

—WILLIAM SHAKESPEARE

Whenever we think of the military, the first image that comes into many people's minds is a combat with death, destruction, and the horrors of battle. However, there are examples of people who had the same purpose and motivation as their fellow servicemen, but they served in a way true to their moral and spiritual purpose.

A fantastic example of that would be Desmond Doss. If you have heard that name before, it is probably because of the famous movie *Hacksaw Ridge*. People like Corporal Doss are very rare; they put their personal beliefs so far above their own safety and conforming to the norms that many people with his moral code of never killing another or even touching a rifle would never succeed in the military. These conscientious objectors would typically never be a good fit for the military. However, Corporal Doss's personal convictions and patriotism allowed him to honor his beliefs while still serving in the Army during some of the most horrific fighting in World War II. People like this leave a legacy of honor, integrity, and service behind that echo in eternity. In this specific case, even Hollywood took notice.

Corporal Doss was a shipbuilder before the war and was even offered a deferment because of his shipyard work but instead, he enlisted in the United States Army. Within three and a half years of service, he found himself receiving the nation's highest award for his bravery and courage under fire, the Medal of Honor. Typically, valor in combat is usually associated with heroic fighting in the face of overwhelming conditions. Almost all Medal of Honor citations list how they took the fight to the enemy while sacrificing their own personal safety. Corporal Doss's citation was different in that he did not take the fight to the enemy like other Medal of Honor recipients, but it was similar in that he disregarded his own safety to help his brother warriors. His purpose was simple, to help people and protect as many lives as possible, and that is exactly what he did.

It all began in 1942 when Desmond Doss joined the United States Army. He was one of the 16 million men who became an active part of the Second World War. Sixteen million is a huge number, and out of these, a mere 431 men in uniform received the Medal of Honor. Desmond Doss happened to be one of those 431. Doss was different from the other 430 recipients of the award. This Seventh-Day Adventist Christian refused to use or even carry a gun to kill anyone. He understood his purpose was to serve people and save people. Instead of killing others and defending himself and accomplishing his mission through killing the enemy, he chose to defend his fellow soldiers using his skills as a medic. Corporal Doss was using his faith and purpose rather than a rifle and grenades. He honored his purpose and his own set of morals and served with honor, courage, and selfless sacrifice.

In the process, Doss was assigned to an infantry rifle company where his refusal to carry any sort of weapon or means of destruction caused him trouble. But what's a warrior without challenges he works to overcome? All the men around him tried to put him down for the approach he took. His was a new perspective others in a traditional war scenario wouldn't appreciate, but he held his own. He was bullied and called names. In fact, his commanding officers began to see him as a liability, in the beginning, owing to his gentle southern tone and skinny build. They couldn't imagine a soldier and a frontline warrior without a weapon.

There was bullying, scolding, threatening, and even an attempt at a court-martial for him for refusing the direct order of carrying weapons. Corporal Doss persevered through all of these obstacles. The effect of Doss's purpose was so strong that when President Harry S. Truman was presenting him the Medal of Honor, he warmly held his hand and told him he considered awarding Doss the highest award for courage and valor, which is a bigger honor than being president of the United States.

Throughout his journey, especially during the World War, he served in combat on the islands of Guam and Leyte, where his teammates were taking lives and he was saving them. Bullets and mortar shells took over the physical and mental space around the soldiers, but Doss ran from one fallen comrade the other, carrying them back to life and safety. As they reached Okinawa, Doss had already been awarded two Bronze Stars for his bravery and resilience.

In May, the same year, there was a sudden attack by the Japanese forces on the American target, Maeda Escarpment. The soldiers would refer to it as the Hacksaw Ridge. More than a hundred soldiers were wounded and dying on Japanese soil. During this time, the one lone warrior, the one defiant of his commanders, rose to the occasion. Doss rescued many of the same soldiers who had once called him names when he refused to take up arms. He vowed to rescue as many as he possibly could until his last breath. In the process, he saved at least seventy-five lives that day. It was the fifth of May, his Sabbath. After this, many Americans were taken back down the escarpment, but Doss stayed. He chose to stay with the wounded when no one else did. He was fulfilling his purpose the way he wanted to.

Desmond Doss and his heroics didn't end here. The battle was still ongoing, and Doss was severely wounded in the leg. However, he chose for other people to be treated before him. It is reported he treated himself and waited five hours to be rescued. He acted like a true warrior—putting the team before himself. People who ridiculed him and wanted him out of the forces for being too gentle and too nonviolent soon began to change their opinion. It was because Doss had saved most of their lives.

Captain Jack Glover, one of the commanders who wanted Desmond Doss out, was ironically saved by him in the middle of the battle.

"He was one of the bravest persons alive, and then to have him end up saving my life was the irony of the whole thing."

—CAPTAIN JACK GLOVER

Doss was a courageous man with a purpose that made him change everything around him for the better. When we talk about a warrior, it typically means someone with all the traits we have previously discussed throughout the book. Each one of those, and maybe even more, apply to Corporal Doss. He stood by his principle, had a unique purpose, and acted upon it despite all the hurdles that came his way.

At this point, you may be asking yourself, *How is this related to entrepreneurs?* The purpose, commitment, and motivation doesn't just apply to situations like a war with death and destruction, but also to the world of business and commerce. Let's shift gears a little bit and look at an entrepreneur who made a huge change spurred by a profound purpose.

IT ALL STARTED WITH A MOUSE

You would be hard pressed to find someone who wasn't a fan of Mickey Mouse. Just a few clips of those time-honored music or cartoons can bring a smile to your face even after a bad day. Few people have experienced the happiest place in the world, Disneyland, and not have it bring back childhood memories of joy while absorbing the magic in their children's faces. Walt Disney and his purpose of making people happy was the driving purpose behind this magical place. He chose to turn his purpose into a business idea. He failed many times and even lost work. But he was a true entrepreneur and a true warrior and never gave up on his purpose of making others happy.

> "When you believe in a thing, believe in it all the way, implicitly and unquestionable."
>
> —WALT DISNEY

What Disney achieved is nothing short of a heroic feat we must understand and draw inspiration from. Today, his contribution to cartoons, movies, theme parks, and the overall idea of wholesome family entertainment remains unparalleled. For him, making people happy by tapping into their rusting imaginations and making them dream of bigger and happier things was the purpose. To date, Mickey Mouse and Donald Duck are spreading joy to children and teenagers alike while also catering to family audiences. I remember visiting Disney World several years ago with my family. As we waited in line for the ride "Peter Pan's Flight," I felt myself brought back to that magical time as a kid when I really thought Peter Pan would visit me and make me fly. As the ride lifted off in darkness and I could see the lights of the city of London below, I felt so much happiness that I actually had to hold back tears of joy.

It wasn't just the movies that Disney made or the cartoons he created, but it was also the idea of theme parks that he revolutionized with Disneyland. This theme park was built for people to have an exciting environment where they could have fun and relax. He created a world full of dreams and happiness. He helped people believe in dreams, imagination, and positivity again.

The Walt Disney Company started in 1923 as a rather basic cartoon studio. Today, it is operational in more than forty countries as an international media conglomerate. As of 2019, it employs around 223,000 individuals currently and over $200 billion in total assets. This is a prime example of how purpose turned into a business that touches all corners of the world.

The countless stories of purpose make for excellent business motivation. I have heard and read all about these phenomenal gamechangers, and I have also experienced it firsthand in my life. When I read about such stories and how people driven by purpose managed to achieve everything they did, in terms of creating and growing a business and purpose, I wasn't sure if I could create something similar. However, my experiences had shaped my purpose. I then acted on it to make things better not just for myself but for my fellow firefighter warriors who I would never want to get lost and disoriented in a dark and smoke-filled structure.

Being a firefighter, like other warriors, means putting others above your own safety and comfort. Any job where you put your life second to strangers is an occupation of honor. In my experience as a firefighter, as we have talked about earlier in the book, I had a life-threatening experience that changed my outlook and the way I perceived the job I was doing. I still remember that day in the fire, when I became lost from the blacked-out smoke conditions. It wasn't just fear; it was a primal fear of both darkness and a claustrophobic feeling that made me feel like I may not survive. Breathing seemed like a chore as I knew I was running low on air. Panic started to set in, and I could not think. However, I knew failure was not an option, and I reverted to my training. Eventually, I managed to egress the building to the safety of the outside. In a way, this event made me a different person.

It was my experience and empathy for my brother and sister firefighters who have in the past and in the future gone through similar conditions when the dark smoke disoriented them that shaped my purpose of solving this problem. I wanted to make sure no other firefighter ever feels the way I did that day. As a result of the purpose that I had then, and still do, I developed my lighting product that solved a particular problem for the firefighters and helped them not just do their job better, but also keep themselves safe. Moreover, the safer they remain themselves, the more chances they will save people around them. Today, my purpose and dedication have led to almost 100,000 firefighters around the world using my product.

If you begin to research it, you will find plenty of statistics and case studies about how purpose-driven businesses are doing exceptionally well today. Statistics do motivate some people to take giant strides into learning and acting. However, one also needs to remember the purpose has to come from within. It has to be something you know you feel strongly about and really want to achieve.

Our stories in this chapter aren't just statistics. These are real experiences and rewards. That is why it is vital to know success stories of warriors and entrepreneurs who try to shape the world and make it a little better.

Find a purpose you want to channel your energy toward. Make sure you give it the dedication it deserves. Be a warrior in the way you tackle all the obstacles that come your way, and allow nothing to stop you from your mission. Failure and disappointment are never the end; they are just minor setbacks that can be both overcome and learned from.

THE WHY

In the previous part of this chapter, we talked thoroughly about what it means to have a purpose. It is great to have a purpose and to know how far it can take us. Where earlier, we focused on meaningful examples of how purpose is the steppingstone toward the top, now we will explore the theory of purpose and the idea of "WHY."

I will discuss the "WHY" under the light of Simon Sinek's explanation. Let me ask this question: *What is why?* "WHY" is the sole reason behind the actions you take, whether in your business or personal life. This "WHY" will always be the answer to many questions you ask yourself and others.

For example, why do you think you get out of bed every morning? The answer will be to make a difference in the world for some people, while others would say it's to have a good time. The "WHY" will always vary but will be omnipresent in all your successes.

This doesn't just hold true for a businessperson; it is also true for consumers. This fact can help a businessperson tailor their products and services. By simply understanding the "WHY" of consumers, a businessperson understands a consumer's purpose; they understand what the consumer values. This allows the business to utilize the "WHY" to effectively serve the consumer.

It is all linked if you think about it. Simon Sinek talks about how Apple has made it to the top by understanding what its competitors have failed to do. The "WHY" of Apple is to challenge the status quo and empower individuals. This has created an aura around Apple being authentic and close to individuality. Sinek explains that if Apple advertised like others, they would say something like, "We make great computers. They're beautifully designed, simple to use, and user friendly. Want to buy one?"

Instead, according to Sinek, Apple tells us:

> *"Everything we do, we believe in challenging the status quo. We believe in thinking differently. The way we challenge the status quo is by making our products beautifully designed, simple to use and user friendly. We just happen to make great computers. Want to buy one?"*

Here's another aspect of the "WHY," as Simon Sinek explains. He talks about how human nature has an undying desire to belong to something or someone. As a result, they look for people who share the same "WHY" as them and then collaborate with them. Let's take this a notch higher and involve a little bit of biology. The human system has a neo-cortex. The neo-cortex deals with us according to our "WHAT." This helps us analyze, but doesn't quite drive, our behavior.

What drives our behavior is our limbic brain, which captures our feelings, trust, and loyalty. It is in this instinctual part of the brain that our "WHY" happens. We are not just socially but biologically inclined toward people and organizations who share the same purpose as us. This works fantastically well for all businesspersons. As entrepreneurs or warriors, when you tap into your purpose, you create a tribal sense of belonging to a similar "WHY." You let the customers and fellow warriors know you care about their "WHY," and you join them on their mission.

According to Sinek, "the "WHY" does not come from looking ahead at what you want to achieve and then figuring out an appropriate strategy to get there. It is not born out of market research or, for that matter, even extensive interviews with customers or employees. It comes from looking in the opposite direction from where you are right now. Finding the "WHY" is a process of discovery, not invention."

Once you have found the "WHY," the first concern you will have is, "Okay, now what? I have a purpose, and I am prepared to work my way around it, but is that all I need?" The answer is no. You need to keep updating your "WHY" over time. This doesn't mean you change the purpose of your idea or motivation completely; instead, you must modify it year by year. Keep your purpose aligned with your business and fundamental concept. There is no other way around it.

FINAL HONORS

Master Sergeant Adam Green, The Air Force Concert Band, The White House, Washington, DC

Everyone knows the Arlington Cemetery is where many veterans and heroes call their final resting place. This sacred place is very close to the hearts of their fellow military veterans, families, and also its citizens. When there is a burial in a military cemetery, a traditional military funeral ceremony is conducted. It may be as modest as just a lone bugler playing "Taps" and a small honor guard folding the US flag from the casket and presenting it to the next of kin with the appreciation of a grateful nation. As the rank of the deceased is higher, the final honors they merit will become more significant and more involved for the funeral procession and ceremony. More servicemen will participate in the ceremony. They could include drummers, a full military band, horse drawn caissons, and other honors depending on the hierarchy of the rank.

Each of the services has a premier band stationed in Washington, DC. These are usually made up of very talented musicians who could play in most professional orchestras. For the US Air Force, their premier band is the Air Force Concert Band. Sometimes, when the Ceremonial Brass or other military bands cannot participate in the Arlington Funeral for specific reasons, the US Air Force Concert Band will supplement the detail to make sure the fallen hero receives the funeral they have earned. Typically, the procession parade goes through the cemetery to the site of the grave, and the duration and distance of the march vary depending on where the person is to be buried and their rank.

This is a logistically planned procession. With these planning logistics, a backup plan will always be accounted for. These backup plans need to come into action in a few rare cases, but the most obvious one is major temperature extremes.

For example, temperatures rising over 102 degrees, or going below thirty-two degrees, will lead to larger parades being downgraded to nothing but a bugler and a drummer, to ensure the safety of anyone and everyone involved.

So, one day, a high-ranking general was set to be laid to rest. But the Ceremonial Brass was occupied with something else, and the US Air Force Band supplemented the sixteen-member funeral processional parade. Master Sergeant, Adam Green, a percussionist with the US Air Force Band, reached the ready room to practice and prepare for the procession with his fellow US Air Force Concert Band members. All of them grouped to watch the weather details to determine if the full honors would be rendered or be downgraded to just a bugler. The deteriorating frigid weather made it clear that the procession would have to proceed with only a drummer and a bugler.

Master Sergeant Green was preparing to head home when he reflected on his mission and the "why" of honoring his fellow warriors. He stopped and looked around. He saw all his other band members packing up to leave, and then, he looked at all the headstones of all the heroes he had known from many generations. He felt something. He realized that even though the conditions were terrible, they were not bad enough to stop him from accomplishing the mission to honor his fellow brother in arms. He decided he was going to volunteer for the two-person band even though the weather conditions were becoming dangerous.

On a normal bad weather day, Green would be happy about taking a day off, but he knew he was serving a higher purpose this particular day. There was no way he would leave such a high-ranking officer's farewell to someone else. He decided he wanted to be an active part of honoring his brother warrior regardless of the challenges the weather would provide.

Master Sergeant Green stepped out into the blizzard and snow and watched all the white snowflakes gently disappear in the background of all the white headstones. The dignity, respect, and honor made the cold disappear. Master Sergeant Green wanted to be able to give his fellow airman the funeral he deserved. There is no higher purpose in the military than honoring your brothers and sister warriors both in life and in death.

Master Sergeant Adam Green, The Air Force Concert Band,
Arlington National Cemetery, Arlington, VA

CHAPTER 9

CONFIDENCE

——

"If you hear a voice within you say 'you cannot paint,' then by all means paint, and that voice will be silenced."

—VINCENT VAN GOGH

Confidence isn't just a word. Confidence is the means of achieving your purpose. Once you have found your purpose, the next step is always to become confident about it.

Your confidence may come from your belief in your ideals and morals, or it could come from your firm grasp on whatever you wish to do. However, it has to spring from somewhere within for you to become a victorious warrior or entrepreneur.

Let's explore the parallel between warriors and entrepreneurs and how they both use their confidence to become the best people they wish to become.

In the competitive world we live in today, people intimidate us into believing they are better than us. Sure, there might be a few who do our jobs better, but that doesn't mean we are any less than them—it just means they do a good job. There is always room for improvement. We can always get better. Having this faith is the confidence that will take us further in life. Interestingly, this holds true for our professional as well as personal life. Confidence is the key to all the doors that seem locked at the beginning of our journey. Make use of this key in whichever profession you choose to enter, but particularly if you are a warrior entrepreneur.

Let's look at the example of Major Dave Keszei, an inspiring USMC Naval Aviator who flew and commanded F/A-18 Hornets for the US Marine Corps. There are few better examples of warrior confidence than his.

"Confidence is preparation; everything else is beyond your control."

—RICHARD KLINE

Naval Aviator Dave Keszei, USMC (second from left)

In the military, few people are more certain of their abilities than those elite warriors of the air who earn the right to wear the coveted Naval Aviator Wings.

Due to lack of education, obesity, and other physical problems, or criminal history, about 25 percent of seventeen- to twenty-four-year-olds are even fit enough to serve in the military. About 400,000 individuals serve in the US Navy, and another 220,000 serve in the US Marine Corps. Of these approximately 620,000 individuals, there are about 3,700 manned aircraft between the two branches. This means there are fewer than 0.006 percent available slots for sailors and marines who want to earn the coveted gold Naval Aviator Wings.

All Marines, be they officers or enlisted, are combat warriors first. Every Marine is trained to be an infantry rifleman before they attend any occupational training. For US Marine Corps officers, this usually includes ten to twelve weeks of

Officer Candidate School, where up to 50 percent wash out. It is followed by a rigorous six-month initial training at The Basic School.

At The Basic School in the hills of Quantico, Virginia, Marine officers learn how to be competent infantry commanders by learning the essentials of leading combat Marines. Mission accomplishment takes precedence over everything, including troop welfare.

Once these Marine Officers graduate from the Basic School, they then attend their respective Marine Corps military occupational specialties. In the case of Naval Aviators, one of the longest and most difficult occupational training schools. This begins with six weeks of Aviation Preflight Indoctrination in Florida, followed by twenty-two weeks of Primary Flight Training in Florida, Texas, or Oklahoma, and then fourteen to twenty-nine weeks of Advanced Flight Training in Florida, Mississippi, or Texas. After all of this rigorous training, which about only one out of five will complete, the US government will have invested about $1,000,000 in each pilot.

The coveted backbone of Marine Corps fighter jets is the F/A-18 Super Hornet. It can fly at several times the speed of sound and has the ability to attack targets in the air, land, and sea. If you combine this with the difficulty of landing on an aircraft carrier, it becomes one reason why Naval Aviators, especially Marines, exude the confidence that comes with that training and responsibility.

US Marine Corps Naval Aviator Major Dave Keszei shares that the difficulty of being an aviator isn't about *how* to fly the fighter jets, but instead is processing information. The ability to process information quickly is what sets Aviators like him apart. For him, the basics of flying are very straightforward. But things get a little more challenging when flying a fighter jet because of the speeds and how quickly things can happen when you travel faster than a bullet.

Taking those challenges and landing your fighter jet on an aircraft carrier in the middle of the ocean can be overwhelming and nerve-wracking. This is especially the case because the landing strip looks like a postage stamp floating in the sea when you are thousands of feet above, operating a complex aircraft like the F/A-18 Hornet.

The need to manage multiple systems, plan missions, use your aircraft as a vehicle and a weapon for both air-to-air and air-to-ground combat situations is one of the reasons it is so incredibly challenging to be a Naval Aviator. Moreover, it includes simultaneously correctly handling emergencies and being responsible for leading your team. It isn't just the skill; the role also demands a tremendous amount of confidence.

Let's look deeper into what makes Major Keszei's confidence an example and source of inspiration. He says that regardless of the many technical aspects of flying, four main attributes separate warrior aviators from just aircraft pilots:

1. The ability to rapidly process tremendous volumes of information.
2. The ability to compartmentalize and rapidly prioritize information.
3. The ability to immediately adapt to and overcome any situation.
4. The ability to debrief and handle constructive criticism with humility and authenticity.

A perfect example of how these four attributes came together was in the 1980s during a blue water operation in the Arabian Sea. Blue water operations mean there is no opportunity to reach land on a single tank of fuel. These are very challenging and complicated, as there are no diverts (routing to another location than the original destination) other than the aircraft carrier.

Blue water operations are a capability unique to the US Navy. That gives them a definite advantage; very few other countries can conduct these operations anywhere in the world covered by 71 percent water. There are no diverts, and there are virtually no contingency plans if something goes wrong.

In this case, Major Keszei and his fellow task force were over 500 miles from India's coast. For this mission, twenty-one jets with live missiles were conducting nighttime operations when they flew into a dangerous storm. This storm created high winds, large waves, and limited visibility, all leading to some of the worst conditions possible, creating a nightmare scenario for landing on the aircraft carrier.

The sea had twenty- to forty-foot waves causing the carrier to encounter a double pitching deck. This meant at any time, the landing deck of the aircraft carrier could almost instantly drop or rise forty feet. In addition to the up and down movement of the aircraft carrier's landing strip, it also rolls from side to side by up to forty feet. Landing in these conditions becomes especially complicated by night due to a lack of light and limited visibility from the storm. As Major Keszei stated, "It doesn't get more difficult than this, but this is what you train for."

The twenty-one aircrafts were operating with live missiles; the F/A/18 Super Hornets were armed with the lethal A-9 sidewinders, and AIM-7 Sparrows and the F-14s Tomcats had the massive Phoenix long-range air to air missiles.

As all the jets funneled up into the landing pattern, to begin to land on the deck of the aircraft carrier, Maj. Keszei began to run through the landing procedures in his mind. He was second to land out of the twenty-one, behind his wingman, the F-14 Tomcat, who was making the final approach onto the landing strip of the aircraft carrier.

Suddenly, the blackness of the night was violently filled with a bright orange and red explosion. The aircraft carrier was engulfed in flames. This meant only one thing: The worst-case scenario had happened. His wingman had crashed. As the radio traffic took on a tense and fevered pitch, Maj. Keszei realized his fellow aviator, his wingman, was dead, and the only place he and his nineteen other aviators could land was on fire.

Landing on an aircraft carrier requires consideration of precise angles and altitudes. The margin of error can be measured in inches versus a typical ground-based landing strip where the margin of error can be measured in hundreds of feet. The landing strip of the aircraft carrier had been pitching up, down, and sideways. When the F-14 landed, the deck had risen abruptly, causing the Tomcat to strike the front edge of the aircraft carrier and crash in half. The backseat pilot was automatically ejected, and the pilot perished in the explosion.

As the radio traffic shifted to fight the fire, Maj. Keszei flew over the deck to assess the situation for his fellow aviators who still needed to land. The deck was engulfed in flames. To make matters worse, he could see that one of the live Phoenix missiles was on the deck surrounded by fire. He knew that if this missile detonated, it could sink the entire aircraft carrier. Maj. Keszei later found out that four brave sailors heroically ran through the flames and lifted the missile, dumping it overboard into the sea.

If Maj. Keszei and his other nineteen jets could not make it to safety, they would cause the single largest naval aviation disaster since WWII. He had to start running through his options, and he had to do it quickly. Through all the chaos of the crash and subsequent fire, the commander had the foresight to launch a fuel tanker. This would allow the fighter jets that were already low on fuel to give them a little more time in the air as the aircraft carrier crew put out the fire.

One option was to take that extra fuel and divert all the jets to India about 500 miles away. When the Indian military realized they might have twenty fully armed fighter jets "invade" their sovereign space, they let the carrier know that they would reluctantly allow the planes to land. However, they also made it clear that once the twenty fully armed fighter jets were on Indian soil, they would seize the jets as a spoil of war.

The option to divert to India was not a possibility. As Maj Keszei and the other pilots discussed the next course of action, they realized their options were limited to only one: land on the carrier. Major Keszei shared, "Even though there are no options, there are always options." This lack of options provides clarity; you realize all your focus is consumed with that single option.

Since their fuel was limited, they again lined up for landing, but there would be no second pass on this attempt. In the naval aviation world, this is called trick or treat. You either land or you eject. Major Keszei knew that if he ejected, he would be landing in twenty-to-forty-foot waves at nighttime. The survival rate on ejections is very low at these altitudes, and the chance of successful recovery in the dark ocean during a storm like this was around 10 to 20 percent. Maj. Keszei stated it was straightforward—you're either going to make this landing on this deck, or you're going to die trying.

He and his fellow Naval Aviators focused on their training and controlled emotions, and they executed their mission. One by one, each jet lined up with the damaged runway of the aircraft carrier and landed. Major Keszei couldn't control that he just lost his wingman, he couldn't control the twenty-to-forty-plus-foot swells and pitching deck, and he couldn't control the conditions, but he could control himself and execute his mission. He processed all the information that resulted in those conditions. He compartmentalized and prioritized that information, and he adapted and overcame the challenges of his situation. He had confidence in his plan, in his training, and the warrior ethos of the Marine Corps.

VMFA- 321, Marine Fighter Attack Squadron 321 "Hells Angels"

As the ancient emperor and philosopher Marcus Aurelius once said, "The more we value things outside our control, the less control we have." This is because as a warrior you need to rapidly process information you can control. There is no reason to waste time, energy, and thought on areas you can't change or control.

Being an entrepreneur is like flying an airplane. There are many gauges that an entrepreneur needs to always monitor. If you focus on one gauge, you may miss the other gauges. For example, if you only look at your Airspeed Indicator, you may miss what your Altitude Indicator is telling you and you could crash into the ground. You could start to climb instead of descending. If you only focus on what your altimeter says, you may not have enough speed, and you could stall. As an entrepreneur, speed is your ability to pivot and execute; altitude can be your cash flow. The more cash an entrepreneur has the more opportunity they have to recover from a mistake. Running out of cash is like running out of altitude—both end up in a crash! A good business plan needs to take all of these gauges into account, but you also have to monitor them continuously.

Before you can use any of the gauges to work, you need to take off. Without an adequate runway, no airplane can take off. In business, your runway is cash, and the amount of cash you have determines how long your runway will be. For a plane to fly, it needs something to propel it forward—that's the engine. But for an engine to work, it needs fuel. In a business, fuel is cash. As the saying goes, "Cash is king." The number one reason most businesses fail is that they run out of cash. Businesses can obtain cash from founders, customers, or investors. Cash is crucial to a business' survival just as fuel is critical for an airplane to fly.

We must understand that where fuel and other mechanics of an airplane are integral, so is the confidence needed to operate all of this. If Major Keszei didn't have confidence, we wouldn't have him as a phenomenal example today. He showed confidence in his skill, and he showed confidence in himself and everything he had learned.

TURNING DISADVANTAGES INTO ADVANTAGES

Look around you; you probably have lights on in your room, your family is somewhere around the kitchen, with fancy spotlights on the ceiling, and if you peek out of the window, you see streetlights at work. If one man didn't have confidence, then the world might not be a brightly lit place. Yes, we are talking about Thomas Edison!

The awe-inspiring story of Thomas Edison lighting the world up with his talent, skill, and undeniable confidence. Today, Edison is looked upon as one of the world's greatest inventors. Electric power is one of his most prized inventions, and to date, it powers most of the things we use.

At the age of seven, Edison moved to Port Huron in Michigan with his family and attended school for three months. The teachers at his school struggled to relate to the way he thought and comprehended things. They dismissed him, questioning his mental capabilities. He was withdrawn from his school and educated at home for quite some time. He was a genius, and geniuses particularly those with exceptional thinking capabilities that exceed the limits of a normal human being, are often isolated.

When Edison was a child, a particular incident at a train station impacted his future work.

"A trainman reached over and grabbed me by the ears and lifted me...I felt something snap inside my head and the deafness started from that time and has progressed ever since....Earache came first, then a little deafness, and this deafness increased until at the theatre I could hear only a few words now and then."

—THOMAS EDISON

However, he didn't let this obstacle stop him from working hard. With confidence, he achieved everything he aimed to.

He had met a challenge, but because he had confidence in himself, he encountered it head on. Edison began working on creating devices that would eventually help things get easier and possible for him, despite his deafness. The first was a printer that could convert electrical signals to letters using electricity to signal dashes and dots.

This was possible because of his undying confidence in himself and the fact that he knew he was meant to do it, come what may. As the world stands today, we can't help but be inspired by Thomas Edison, who made some of the world's best inventions.

"I never quit until I get what I'm after. Negative results are just what I'm after. They are just as valuable to me as positive results."

—THOMAS EDISON

Edison never gave up and worked the hardest to achieve all the goals he set for himself over time. If the results were negative once, he would try again, and then work harder and get a positive outcome. Even when he lost his hearing, he didn't use it as an excuse to fail. Instead, he used that to his advantage as he could concentrate better on his work and research.

This is the mindset of a confident person looking for ways to change their disadvantage to their advantage. This is also what we see warriors do, be it on the battlefield or in the office. Warriors work to create the best out of whatever disadvantages they face. Warriors use their confidence to turn their disadvantages into advantages and then triumph.

Edison and Major Keszei both have incredible stories of confidence and resilience to tell. I looked at them for inspiration as I used confidence to overcome many of my struggles. One particular event that really tested my confidence was when I was looking to raise venture capital. Getting people to put their money in an idea that has yet to come to fruition is one of the biggest and most frequent challenges that entrepreneurs face. Some face it earlier in their journey while others come to it later. But rest assured, every entrepreneur experiences this uncertainty.

It takes both confidence and resilience to work through the challenges that come from VC firms or individuals that explore investing. Investors can be brutal with their questions and due diligence. There is a reason the TV show is called "Shark Tank." Investors can be like sharks, always looking for their next prey and taking advantage of the weak and injured.

Raising capital when you have a problem and lack confidence can make the deal very one-sided in the favor of the investors. However, I was strong enough to keep that confidence intact and eventually get where I wanted to. I had a great idea, and our business proposal and pitch deck were well laid out and financially sound. These venture capitalists are looking to rip you apart and tear you to a point where they can see whether or not you have the potential to not only get them their money back but to return it in multiples. For them, it is less about the business idea, but more about the person who is making promises of returns to them.

I was raising millions of dollars to execute the business plan my team and I put together. So, it made sense that investors wanted to gauge me in every way possible. Some made fun of me to my face, and some did it as soon as I walked out of the room, but I knew I couldn't let my confidence down. I had to have the confidence to stand up to them and believe in my purpose. Some just saw the childish fascination with things that glow in the dark, but I had to have the confidence to let them know this could save the lives of the heroes who protect us.

Most of my confidence came from my fraternity of fire-fighters who would continue to tell me how my product was helping them and saving their lives. This kept me going. It fulfilled my purpose and boosted my confidence, telling me I was on the right track. By the time we finished talking to several investors, we had multiple firms interested in funding us, thereby letting us choose what deal was best rather than settling on a single one-sided deal.

The very difference between quitting and never giving up is confidence. This is what I preach to every budding entrepreneur as well. Be confident, and do not let the people around you or situations around you bring you down. As the great basketball coach Jerry West once said, "Confidence is a lot of this game or any game. If you don't think you can, you won't."

CHAPTER 10

TENACITY

"The measure of intelligence is the ability to change."

—ALBERT EINSTEIN

Adapting to change is one of the most integral aspects of human nature. If it weren't for adaptation, the world would have been different, and to be fair, quite absurd. The history of civilization is the history of adaptation.

The world was once a world of kingdoms, with authoritarian rule over every part of the world, and then came the idea of government and people's choice. There was adaptability in this system across the globe. Similarly, wars and warriors have had to adapt to newer ways, technologies, and other ways of fighting.

Back in the day, war meant a brutal hand to hand fight with swords and spears until one side surrendered or fled. If we look at war today, the fighting for the most part has shifted from swords and spears to technology, economy, and advanced weapons that can be deployed from outer space.

The only thing that has remained constant is the need for warriors to adapt to their situation. During wars, warriors need to adapt quickly to prevail. For example, if the weapon of choice malfunctions in the middle of the war, there has to be quick adaptability to the next weapon in hand or field modifications to make it work.

That's how the warrior can succeed. This is also the case for entrepreneurs who are true warriors. They need to adapt to the situation and make the best of it.

As we talk about adaptability, let's look at some inspirational stories we can all learn from. I want to focus on adaptability more because the world recently saw a pandemic, which caused many businesses to take a significant hit they weren't expecting. Adaptability comes in handy at times like these. I did it for my business too, but before we talk about my experience, I would like to share another experience regarding a friend of mine.

President George Bush with Andrew Ciafardini, Oval Office,
The White House, West Wing, Washington DC

This is the story of Andrew Ciafardini. Andrew grew up in
the Cincinnati suburbs of Blue Ash and Montgomery. While
in the early years of college at the University of Cincinnati, he
wrote a letter to then-Texas Governor George W. Bush asking
if he could help with his upcoming presidential campaign.
When Andrew received a handwritten letter back telling him
to "keep the powder dry," he never knew where that would
lead.

A few months later, he had accepted a job as an advance
team representative for the Bush 2000 campaign. He was
traveling all over the USA as a staff member of the soon to
be the forty-third president of the United States.

Andrew never thought he'd be serving his country in the
nation's capital, let alone the White House. That's where
Andrew's first job was once President Bush won the 2000

election. He quickly became a rising star in the Presidential Administration and was assigned to the office of the US Secretary of State after only a few short months. Andrew had no idea what lay ahead in the coming months. He didn't know that this move would soon place him in the center of a high stakes global mission on behalf of the President of the United States.

For almost twenty years, a brutal civil war in Sudan took many lives as fighting raged between the Muslim north and the Christian South. President Bush decided something needed to be done, and he named USAID Administrator Natsios as a special envoy to Sudan. Through Administrator Natsios's leadership and diplomacy with all the parties in Sudan, a fragile peace was brokered. The plan was to have representation from the South by having former SLPA rebel leader John Garang as the joint country's first vice president.

Vice President Garang helped the southerners who felt oppressed and marginalized by the government in the capital of Khartoum. After decades of brutal fighting, Sudan was starting to come together through Vice President Garang's leadership and the work bridging the gap between the Muslims and Christians. This would all soon change when Vice President Garang and thirteen others were killed when their helicopter crashed in bad weather returning from Uganda.

Immediately, the southern Sudanese believed the crash was intentional and he was assassinated by members of their government. Because of the distrust between the northern Muslims and the southern Christians, the accusation of helicopter sabotage took off through the country, quickly destroying the fragile peace. People were pulled off public buses and executed in the streets. Tensions flared, and in the chaotic following days, hundreds were killed. The beginning of a new civil war seemed imminent. Riots started to break out all over Sudan, and the Muslims in the South were flowing into the north in preparation for war.

The United States had to do something to salvage the peace they had worked so hard to achieve. That afternoon, an urgent cable from the White House came across Andrew's desk at the State Department. It was a memo that directed him to assemble a mission to Sudan. A mission that activated a series of harrowing events that no one could have ever anticipated. Tenacity, adaptability, grit, and risk would be required to complete this critical mission Andrew was tasked to execute. Global implications and thousands of lives would be on the line.

Upon hearing of Vice President Garang's death and the subsequent escalations of hostilities, President Bush named USAID Administrator Andrew Natsios to personally represent him at the funeral to help quell the unrest. By President Bush sending a high-level US representative to the funeral, a clear message would be sent to the Sudanese people that the United States stood by its commitment to the peace agreement. Andrew and the US Department of State were tasked with making this happen.

Typically, a trip of this magnitude would take months to prepare. Andrew had forty-eight hours to put together the logistics, diplomacy, and planning for this presidential delegation to attend the funeral in Sudan. The delegation had to be planned and "wheels up" nearly immediately to meet the timelines required to attend this funeral on the other hemisphere.

Andrew's first challenge was to arrange transportation from the US Air Force to make this multi-continent journey. Since it was such short notice, all of the long-range aircraft were already tasked with other missions, and Andrew's only option was a mid-range jet that did not have the range to make it to Sudan without several refueling stops along the way.

Nevertheless, Andrew secured a team, and pre-flight considerations were started. The Air Force team included a C-20 (Gulfstream III) jet, two pilots, and two Phoenix Ravens. The Phoenix Ravens are a little-known team of elite security commandos highly trained to protect aircraft and crews from enemy assaults while on the ground in dangerous locales. Their only job is to protect the Air Force property and pilots. As Andrew would later find out, they do not provide security for the passengers.

Next, Andrew had to get Administrator Natsios to DC. However, the very tight timelines got even more dynamic as they had a difficult securing the central figure for this presidential delegation, Administrator Natsios.

Administrator Natsios was on a personal vacation at Acadia National Park's Swans Island, which is one of a series of remote islands off the coast of Maine. Administrator Natsios likely cherished his time on the primitive island because he could completely go off the grid. There was no electricity, no mobile coverage, no connections to the modern world, very little ability for anyone to reach him consistently.

Working through Natsios' chief of staff in DC, Andrew was told that he himself had limited contact with the Administrator and the only way we could get him to DC the next morning to fly out of Andrews Air Force Base (now called Joint Base Andrews) was to get him off the island by boat to the Portland, Maine airport. The problem—only one ferry the next morning and it was fully booked. How would the team get Natsios off the island, to the airport and to Andrews AFB in time? It was nearly midnight in Washington and Natsios needed to be on the 9 a.m. flight to Andrews and if he missed it, the delegation would never make the funeral.

After attempting to reach every car service in Portland and even contacting the local police department, no one was available to help, but the police did suggest that we contact the National Park Service Ranger for Acadia. Andrew and his teammate needed to think creatively and ensure someone took responsibility. And at nearly midnight, Andrew and his team called the lone park ranger at his home and asked him for assitance with a presidential mission to avoid a civil war. This was with out a doubt the craziest request he ever had. Was it a prank? Would he show up at the ferry in the morning to meet Administrator Natsios with a sign and transport him all the way to Portland?

One can only imagine the reaction from that National Park Ranger upon hearing the details of that call. Less than twenty-four hours later, Andrew and the delegation were flying over the North Atlantic in a small ten-seat Air Force jet en-route to Ireland for their first of several refueling stops. Because a long-haul aircraft could not be located on such short notice, they had to fly the smaller C-20 Gulfstream III aircraft whose maximum range was about 4,000 miles. Since they could not make the trip to Sudan directly, timelines had to be adjusted to include several refueling stops.

Andrew Ciafardini in Presidential Motorcade, Undisclosed Location

After the initial refueling stop in Ireland, the crew and the delegation would require a mandatory rest. They overnighted in Egypt, which was the farthest they could fly before taking the required mandatory rest period. The Air Force pilots needed to be fresh when flying into potentially hostile territory.

As Andrew worked the timelines, he realized there was a chance they would land after the funeral if everything didn't stay on time, driven by the Air Force pilots suggesting they leave early. During the mandatory rest for the pilots, Andrew communicated by satellite phone with the few U.S. State Dept personnel on the ground in Sudan and the charge de affaires, who was staying in Kenya to arrange transportation and security once they landed in Sudan. They informed Andrew that since they were short staffed—the only U.S. Diplomatic Security Agents available would be with the other delegation members already in Sudan.

As Andrew's frustration grew, the Phoenix Raven security guard could overhear the conversation. Before Andrew could even complete his sentence to ask for him to provide on the ground security, he explained to Andrew in a respectful but forceful tone that he could not leave the jet. His responsibility laid with the aircraft, pilot, and a steel briefcase that was never farther than arm's reach.

After several hours for their mandatory rest in Cairo, they traveled to their next refueling stop, Khartoum, Sudan. They would need to refuel here before continuing to Juba—their destination—in Southern Sudan. Unlike Egypt, they did not know what to expect once they landed. In fact, because of the situation and emerging conflict the aircraft made a special tactical landing at the airport to avoid the potential of being targeted by a surface to air missile.

After landing, it was then that Andrew saw the Phoenix Ravens go into full action. They left the airplane with their machine guns at the ready. As they waited in the sweltering heat, a 1970s era refueling truck approached the jet, you could feel the tension in the air. Would a local northern Sudanese terrorist element sabotage the aircraft while on the ground? To make matters even more tense, while on the ground and refueling, the Air Force flight engineer spotted a minor mechanical problem that he also quickly repaired.

After a refueling stop in Khartoum, they completed the final miles of this journey, Juba's small runway came into view. It was the only paved aircraft runway in Southern Sudan. However, instead of making the final approach, they were placed into the crowded circling pattern. The skies became more and more crowded with dozens of other diplomatic aircraft bringing in leaders and delegations from all over the world. This small runway was simply not equipped for this volume of traffic all trying to land in time for the funeral. Moreover, it was unclear what was really happening on the ground. Why were most planes not being cleared immediately? From the radio air traffic, there was some concern that another insurrection on the ground was already occurring.

As they circled, the Ravens asked Andrew if he and the civilian delegate had body armor. They did not, but the Ravens offered their extra bullet proof vests to those on board. And as Andrew prepared to give the administrator his bulletproof vest, Administrator Natsios quickly refused. He calmly and confidently stated, "It's not that I'm not concerned about my safety. It's that I'm a skinny guy and if I wear one, the Sudanese will know I'm wearing one, and that will send the wrong signal about our presence here and our work to hold the peace agreement together. They mustn't think I feel unsafe among them." Andrew was floored by his incredible courage amid this very dangerous situation.

After over an hour of circling overhead, Andrew was once again summoned to the cockpit. The pilot's face said it all. Andrew knew it was bad news; he was informed that if they could not land in the next fifteen to twenty minutes, they would need to scratch the mission. They would not have enough fuel. Andrew requested the pilot to share this new development with the aircraft control tower, but they were advised they would have to continue to circle in the holding pattern.

Through the satellite phones on the aircraft, Andrew called through the U.S. Department's Operations Center to be connected with the Assistant Secretary for African Affairs, who was on the ground in Juba. Andrew had to determine if it was indeed actually safe to land and understand how explosive or safe the situation on the ground was. They had come too far, risked too much, and fought through multiple challenges to give up now, but Andrew needed clarity to ensure the mission could be safely executed.

The famous line from Clint Eastwood, who played US Marine Corps Gunnery Sergeant Highway in the movie Heartbreak Ridge, came into play—Andrew and his team had to "improvise, adapt, and overcome." That is precisely what Andrew did.

After running through all the limited options available, the pilot finally informed Andrew that short of an emergency and a mayday landing, there was probably no way they would be able to land their plane before they ran out of fuel. Andrew explained that an emergency was exactly what was happening, as he would not allow them to return without the delegation attending the funeral. A few seconds later, the radio came alive with the emergency mayday message being declared, and their jet was given clearance to land.

The intense heat on the ground matched the intense conditions amongst the people of Sudan. The previous night over one hundred people had been killed near the airport. Andrew needed to arrange security for his team, but they would be on their own. The only arrangement that could be put together for them from the nearby US embassy was an old rickety van with one diplomatic security agent that had come back from the funeral site at the demand of Andrew. The Ravens had to stay with the plane and the pilots, especially if we needed to make a quick evacuation. Once again, Andrew needed to improvise, adapt, and overcome the situation at hand.

As they drove to the funeral site, they were joined by over 5,000 Africans streaming into the outdoor ceremony. As Andrew looked around the outdoor ceremony with over 5,000 in attendance, he reflected on the events of the last few days. As the vice president's widow gave her remarks to all in attendance and the world's television cameras, Andrew was overtaken with emotions on what he heard, he said. She eulogized her husband and went on to thank President Bush and the United States of America for all they did to negotiate the end of their twenty-year civil war. In her broken English, she proclaimed her commitment to continuing her husband's work by sticking by the US peace agreement and how much she appreciated the US delegation making the trip in person.

Andrew looked over at Administrator Natsios, and saw that it had worked. Andrew had accomplished the impossible on behalf of the President of the United States. They had made a difference because of his adaptability and bravery and successfully accomplished his mission on behalf of the President of the United States.

Andrew Ciafardini aboard US Air Force Special Mission Aircraft, near Sudan, Africa

To be successful, you must keep on your toes and be ready for any kind of change that might come your way. We must understand that adapting to both ups and downs is part of being a warrior and an entrepreneur. Where the ups make us happy and confident, we need to always keep the downs in our mind so we can both learn from them and to also appreciate the ups.

ACE OF SPADES

Author Zachary Green (left) and Dr. Hans Mumm Creator of the Iraqi Most Wanted Deck of Cards

Another warrior who showed incredible adaptability and tenacity is Dr. Hans Mumm, PhD, a US Army Intelligence Captain who came up with one of the most brilliant and successful intelligence operations in modern history.

"Here's to the crazy ones. The misfits. The rebels. The troublemakers. The round pegs in the square holes. The ones who see things differently. They're not fond of rules. And they have no respect for the status quo. You can quote them, disagree with them, glorify, or vilify them. About the only thing you can't do is ignore them. Because they change things. They push the human race forward. And while some may see them as the crazy ones, we see genius. Because the people who are crazy enough to think they can change the world, are the ones who do."

—STEVE JOBS

In the military, there are officers and then there are mustang officers. The term mustang refers to a very select group of officers who rose through the enlisted ranks to become commissioned. These officers gain instant respect from their soldiers because the men and women they lead know they have walked in their shoes. Hans Mumm was a mustang who rose through the enlisted ranks for eight years when his commanding officer gave him a direct commission as our military was starting our post-9/11 combat missions. Hans' commander knew he was going to have a very important mission as an enlisted member of the US Army Intelligence community, it would be difficult to change the minds of the Army bureaucratic senior leadership. He knew that if he was going to change the bureaucracy of Army Intelligence, he would need to rebel and push the status quo.

Hans was tasked with helping to execute one of President Bush's missions for Operation Iraqi Freedom: regime change. In order to bring freedom to Iraq and bring Saddam Hussein's evil regime to justice, the first thing that would need to be done is to identify the enemies in power. In traditional Army bureaucracy, a field manual needs to be put together. This was not an option as putting together a typical field manual could take years and at the end of the day the typical soldier finds very little use for a technical bureaucratic document that they would rather use as expensive toilet paper rather than read through hundreds of pages of bureaucratic army jargon. Hans' mission needed to be executed in a matter of days and he did not have time to get bogged down in traditional Army power grabs and endless reviews. The soldiers on the ground had to identify Saddam's henchmen and they needed to do it quickly. The fellow members of Hans' intel group devised a very detailed diagram showing the over fifty members of Saddam's government. The diagram had connecting lines, pictures of their faces and information on what they did in Saddam's government. This highly detailed poster board was so detailed it literally took up the entire wall of their command post. So many faces were connected by so many lines that it looked more like a picture of spilled spaghetti rather than an org-chart. It was highly detailed but in order to read all the names on connecting lines it had to be so large that it would take up an entire wall of the command center. This was a big problem as the information in this form would be very difficult to disseminate and be useful to the brave men and women on the ground clearing buildings and manning checkpoints. Something needed to change in order for Hans' mission to be accomplished.

Hans came up with an idea so brilliant, it would not only affect the outcome of the war but forever live on in military history. The last thing a combat soldier wants is more gear, but as dynamic as combat can be, those moments of frantic chaos are usually punctuated with extreme moments of boredom. Since most electronics can't (or shouldn't) be used in the field, playing cards have always been the friend of the soldier to pass the time. With that idea in mind, Hans came up with an idea that would forever affect history. Hans directed his team to take a few decks of playing cards and start to paste the faces of the fifty-two most wanted members of Saddam's team. His goal was to pass these cards out to the troops in the field so as they killed time playing Spades and other games, they could start to remember the names and faces of Iraq's most wanted. He immediately put the plan into action by passing out these homemade cards to special operators throughout Iraq.

As word started to grow about this new idea for finding the most wanted fugitives in Iraq, the bureaucratic old guard at the pentagon also took notice of this alternative way of enemy identification. When the general in charge of intel finally caught wind of what Hans was doing he immediately wanted the program shut down. This general thousands of miles away from the combat theater assumed he knew better than the men "down range" in theater were doing and he wanted the program shut down immediately and all decks of cards to be destroyed.

Hans did everything he could do to keep this program alive; reports were coming in from the field on how the cards were starting to help round up the members of Saddam's ruling party. Reports were also coming in of situations where the most wanted were being allowed to pass through Army checkpoints because those soldiers manning those check points had not received the visual identification cards prior to allowing the fugitives to pass. The cards were so successful a few of the most wanted started to voluntarily turn themselves in to authorities. When they were being debriefed, they asked one of the Iraqi generals why he would voluntarily turn himself in, the general replied, "My face is on playing cards all over my country. I can no longer go anywhere without someone recognizing my face." Just as Hans exhausted everyone of his resources and felt there was no way he would be able to salvage this brilliant idea, the commander of ground forces held up the ace of clubs on national news. Within a matter of hours, the whole world learned about this incredible project and even the president was proud of what an incredibly effective idea this was to help change the regime of one of our era's most evil dictators.

In the next chapter, I will share my experience of adapting early in my career when I moved from firefighter help to exit signs, having a national contract, and adapting to the COVID-19 pandemic that took the world by storm.

CHAPTER 11

ADAPTABILITY

"You must be shapeless, formless, like water. When you pour water in a cup, it becomes the cup. When you pour water in a bottle, it becomes the bottle. When you pour water in a teapot, it becomes the teapot. Water can drip, and it can crash. Become like water my friend."

—BRUCE LEE

Adapting to different situations is one of the most crucial aspects of being a good entrepreneur and a great warrior. Today, as I narrate how we can be successful, I can't help but emphasize the idea of adaptability. Let's look into my business and how I personally worked on making myself, my products, and business idea adaptable to various situations that came my way.

There is no sustainability without adaptability. If you don't adapt, you will perish. When it came to my business, I started with using glow-in-the-dark technology to help firefighters have a non-electric visual reference point so they could increase visual accountability and reduce disorientation.

As I looked to expand the business, I learned that the same non-electric material that illuminated firefighter accessories could also be used to make exit signs.

These glow-in-the-dark letters on the exit signs glowed bright and long enough that they actually met the same code and regulations that electric exit signs met. All this could be accomplished without the need for costly and environmentally unhealthy batteries, lightbulbs, and electricity.

By this time, my brand and my name were becoming well known in the firefighting community. Firefighters have a natural inclination to help others, and anytime firefighters would think of ways to utilize this material, they would call me. As firefighters would shop around the city for groceries, they noticed that the exit signs weren't working due to electrical issues or dead batteries or lightbulbs. I remembered hearing about glow-in-the-dark egress (exit) signs being used in Europe, and I knew I had a chance to help market this technology in the US. I was ready to adapt, and our team was prepared to grow.

In one case while shopping for their groceries at our nation's largest grocery store chain, the firefighters from a nearby town shared with the store manager that his store had many exit signs that were not working. They explained they were just at the store as customers and not as inspectors. As a courtesy, the firefighters told the manager to fix them prior to their annual inspection in a few months. They then shared this situation with me, and I immediately called the store manager. I explained I was an entrepreneur developing a non-electric glow-in-the-dark exit sign that would never fail and would meet all fire and building codes. I offered to retrofit the entire store with these exit signs at no cost with the understanding that he would introduce me to his superiors at their corporate headquarters just a few miles from my office. He accepted my offer and replied how great the timing was as he had a few firefighters share with him recently that they had several exit signs that needed to be fixed. This resulted in an introduction to the senior facility leaders at the nearby Cincinnati headquarters and ultimately the change in the specifications to use our exit signs in all the new and renovated grocery stores for our nation's second largest retailer and largest grocers, Kroger. It was a bold move by the executives, but they also recognized they had to change the kind of exit signs they used.

"Nobody likes to change. There will always be resistance to change, and there always will be change. And the quicker you get to that, the easier it is. It's not such a difficult thing. If you entrench yourself and go, 'By God, I will not change, I will not have this.' Then, you're a dead man. We're great at adaptability. It's our strongest suit."

—NICK NOLTE

This was huge. This was a big national-level contract I had scored. My company was flying and so was I, but I realized that for me to sustain this growth and invest in enough inventory to keep up with future demand, I would need to raise a couple million dollars of venture capital financing. This further helped my cause, and the business was booming. I went ahead and used that capital to grow my team, hiring new people and making my business into a full-fledged national level business. National, and then international, are often the goals that every ambitious entrepreneur sets. For me, I had made it through that first gate. I had entered the national territory in terms of the market I was looking to capture.

"If you're not stubborn, you'll give up on experiments too soon. And if you're not flexible, you'll pound your head against the wall, and you won't see a different solution to a problem you're trying to solve."

—JEFF BEZOS

Adapting changed the way my business operated and allowed us to grow to serve not just firefighters but also whom they protected. We developed a new brand for the exit signs called LumAware®. As our reputation as leader in photoluminescence safety grew, so did our distribution opportunities. We quickly became one of the more respected brands of The Home Depot by being nominated for three awards and in 2021 being awarded the coveted Master of Innovation award. Additionally, through work with The Home Depot, we won CBRE's (the world's largest commercial real estate firm) Innovation of the Year Award. As our innovation and growth accelerated, we had no idea how all of our world was about to change. It is no hidden fact that COVID-19 has greatly impacted businesses of all kinds. My leadership team and I planned for many different scenarios, but none of us had planned for a global pandemic that would cause the entire global economy and supply chain to come to a grinding halt. I remembered from my USMC warrior training that you always have to be prepared to execute your plan but also have to be prepared for the unexpected.

> "Everybody has a plan until they get punched in the mouth."
>
> —MIKE TYSON

My business hit a massive wall once COVID-19 came into the picture and stay-at-home orders started to come into effect around the US and abroad. Everything changed. Everything stopped. Although initially it seemed like this was one battle I would not survive, we adapted to not only weather the storm but also grow from the opportunity created from this change. I was ready to adapt and change; I just initially didn't know how we would do it. This adaptability helped me not only save my business, reputation, and resources but also prevail during this crisis. As other companies looked for ways to cut costs and "hunker down," I looked for ways to bolster our "why" of innovative safety minded solutions. Around this time, one of the business development managers Steve from The Home Depot, who at the time was our largest distributor of our exit sign products, ran an idea by me that allowed us to adapt our manufacturing to help reduce the spread of this deadly virus.

He asked about our access to plexiglass since he knew we used quarter-inch plexiglass in our exit signs. He was having a difficult time finding this material to make protective barriers that the CDC recommended to use in situations where six-foot social distance was not possible. I quickly had my team reach out to our suppliers and immediately started to buy up as much plexiglass as we could find. At the time, we were aware of eight freighters with raw stock of this type of plexiglass en route to the US mainland. We immediately started to buy as much of that inventory as possible and from what I understood, we had purchase orders for the entire stock of four of those eight freighters. As we started to pre-sell these barriers, our broker contacted us and told us they had to cancel our purchase orders as he was able to sell them to other buyers willing to pay more. Importing can be challenging as you truly don't own inventory until it arrives in the country of destination and clears customs. This allows brokers to cancel lower margin orders and replace them with higher margin orders. Nevertheless, we had to adapt once again. One of our supply chain representatives came up with a brilliant idea to protect our original price and secure future orders. We made a deal that would allow us to keep the original price if we committed to buy future orders. This not only allowed us to protect our margins but also ensured an uninterrupted future supply chain. It was a risk as if there wasn't a future need; we would be stuck with unsellable inventory. We had to take that risk because the alternative of not filling our orders and accomplishing our mission was unacceptable.

LumAware's ClearGuard® Covid Protective Barriers, Photo Credit Michael Snyder

Before we knew it, it is our understanding that we quickly became The Home Depot's largest manufacturer of these lifesaving products. We had the tenacity to weather the challenges of COVID-19 and the adaptability to pivot our production.

The COVID-19 environment has created one of the most chaotic times in our world's history. A warrior can look at chaos and see clarity. This clarity allowed us to identify a need, and we had a solution to help people safely return to work, school, and everyday locations. While many businesses could not or would not adapt to the changing environment, we embraced this change as an opportunity to grow our business and serve the community through COVID safety solutions.

"A man is worked upon by what he works on. He may carve out his circumstances, but his circumstances will carve him out as well."

—FREDERICK DOUGLASS

Since we have spoken about The Home Depot in the chapter, it is only appropriate that we use their success story and learn from their adaptability that turned them from a small hardware store to a company that employs over 500,000 employees and $132 billion dollars of revenue in 2021.

Their story is exciting and tells a great deal about the idea of adaptability. The Home Depot first opened in 1979, when there was nothing like it in the home improvement space. At that point, if someone needed home supplies or hardware, they would have to run to multiple stores to get their job done. The idea of The Home Depot worked like magic, and in 1981, the company went public. The early days, however, were a little troublesome. It certainly would not have come into existence if the founders of Home Depot weren't fired during a corporate bloodbath, as the *Business Insider* likes to call it.

Founders Bernie Marcus and Arthur Blank were fired from a company called Hardy Dan. It was one of the first home improvement retail options in the country at that time. However, the company struggled in the late '70s. The struggle wasn't financial but was the result of poor organization and a lack of focus. As a result, Marcus and Blank were fired. Both of them were devastated at the loss of their highly valuable jobs. However, they looked to adapt to the situation, instead of surrendering to the situation. Marcus had an idea. The idea was a one-stop shop for the do-it-yourself. Today, we see the manifestation of that idea in the standing of 2,200 Home Depot stores across the United States. The two corporate executives decided to open this store in a great space and keep their prices extremely competitive and relatively low.

The business began to flourish. After a year, they found a new retailer, and the founders opened a second store in Atlanta. They adapted to a new city because it offered more. It offered an airport and cheap real estate for them. They managed to get themselves a deal with JCPenney and launched two initial stores around Atlanta. When they launched, the initial response wasn't overwhelming, as is with most businesses worldwide. So, they adapted to this situation as well and thought of a promotional plan. The founders passed out around seven hundred dollars in singles to their children and employees who would go out distributing these and ask people to come in and shop for a dollar.

Eventually, business strategies and low prices began to entice people into the store. That boosted their business. It was a much-needed boost as the two founders constantly adapted to challenging situations and improving things for themselves and their business. In the end, it was primarily word of mouth that made the store a big hit amongst the people. By the end of 1979, The Home Depot had already managed three stores, with 200 employees, and over eighty thousand dollars in sales. At the time, this was huge.

Anyway, for The Home Depot, things came to a point where job applications started flooding into their store. They had to set a rather unusual test for them to make it. The test was that these employees were sent into incredibly busy environments where some associates worked over eighty hours a week to keep the business going. They were evaluated on how they could adapt to a chaotic situation that can be routine for most Home Depot employees. They also adapted to the situation when they realized their customers will need to be led into buying things sometimes. The best way to do that is definitely good customer service. They led by example, and Marcus would himself sometimes walk people to their cars and ask why they were leaving empty-handed. He would facilitate them in every way possible.

It has more or less become a cultural icon of the United States. They could only achieve that because they had the right attitude. When they encountered a tough situation, they never backed out or let things be, or waited until devastation happened. They acted quickly and strongly by being adaptable to whatever situation came their way.

"It is a law of nature we overlook, that intellectual versatility is the compensation for change, danger, and trouble. An animal perfectly in harmony with its environment is a perfect mechanism. Nature never appeals to intelligence until habit and instinct are useless. There is no intelligence where there is no change and no need of change. Only those animals partake of intelligence that have a huge variety of needs and dangers."

—H.G. WELLS

The economic, political, and cultural conditions will never remain static around the world. We certainly have no idea when a pandemic could hit us for a year, and we don't know when technology will update itself. We can't always control what resources and products may be popular one month and not the next. In quickly changing times like these, it is integral for entrepreneurs and their businesses to adapt to situations. If you look around, COVID-19 has changed a lot of things. Businesses are being incredibly creative with their ways of adaptation. They have to because adaptation is the key to the sustainability and long-term success of an entrepreneur and a warrior.

"Life is neither static nor unchanging. With no individuality, there can be no change, no adaptation and, in an inherently changing world, any species unable to adapt is also doomed."

—JEAN M. AUEL

CHAPTER 12

NEVER GIVE UP

"Cowards shrink from challenges, weaklings flee from them, but warriors wink at them."

—MATSHONA DHLIWAYO

Sometimes, the moment things stop going our way, our first reaction is to assume it is all over. Before we can give things a second chance, we decide to give up. This is the antithesis of the warrior mindset. Sometimes life throws us curveballs; sometimes life isn't fair. They can rarely control what happens to you, but you can always control your reactions. What differentiates a warrior from others is the ability to never give up. Life will throw situations, problems, and certain people our way who might convince us to surrender. But the fact remains: We must not give up. Giving up is rarely the solution. It is a rather clichéd thing to say, but those who give up never get to know what could be. Imagine a warrior that surrenders at the first sign of the enemy or one who would retreat at the first sign of hardship or difficulty.

Now imagine the same warrior not giving up; imagine him fighting with every physical, emotional, and spiritual fiber of his being. Even if the war is lost and the warrior doesn't give up, he still returns knowing he never gave up. It is his faith in the cause, the faith in his brothers, the faith in his training that makes the warrior heroic. No matter what the odds, no matter how many people told you something was not possible, you have to have faith in your mission.

"Faith consists in believing when it is beyond the power of reason to believe."

—VOLTAIRE

Life doesn't always give you opportunities when you are ready for them. Sometimes, these opportunities will come to us at our lowest points, where we can't think about anything except abandoning them and giving up. Imagine if General Patton told the Nazis to wait until he could have more tanks, fuel, and men before they started the Battle of the Bulge. Imagine if D-Day Commander General Eisenhower called off the invasion of Normandy after the first waves took heavy casualties. Both in battle and in entrepreneurship, it may be difficult to clearly see the path to victory and success. However, it is impossible to accomplish your mission if you give up after things get difficult and plans don't work as intended.

Lieutenant General Lewis Puller is arguably the most famous and revered US Marine Corps warrior. He is nothing short of an inspiration to me and my fellow Marines, and I am sure the more you learn about him, his example of grit and never giving up will inspire you also.

I could have used many quotes by General Lewis "Chesty" Puller to open this chapter. However, I feel the quote I have used by entrepreneur and philosopher Matshona Dhliwayo describes and summarizes the life and career of the Marine Corps legend, Lt. General Lewis Puller.

Born on June 26, 1898, in West Point, Virginia, Puller was destined for the Marines. All through his childhood and early adulthood, he heard stories of hunting and of the Civil War from his relatives. In 1916, when the border war with Mexico began, Lt. General Lewis Puller tried to join the army. However, he stopped because his mother would not give him the required paternal consent as he was too young to sign up on his own.

He didn't want to give up. Even as a young adult, he always had the quality of character that kept him going. In 1918, Lt. General Lewis Puller, who I will fondly refer to as Chesty throughout the story, went to Virginia Military Institute but he was almost immediately placed on inactive reserve status because of downsizing as a result of the end of the first World War.

For him, nothing was going to stand in the way of him pursuing his dream to be a US Marine warrior. Like other Marines, he wasn't one to give up. Chesty wanted to go where all the fighting was. So, he quickly rejoined the Marines as an enlisted man and was sent off to the Gendarmerie d'-Haiti. For over five years, he participated in over forty combat engagements against the Caco rebels in Nicaragua. Chesty fought in multiple battles ranging from Nicaragua to World War II to Korea.

Eventually, he retired from the Marines after thirty-seven years of service. He reached the rank of Lieutenant General and was the most decorated Marine in history. His heroics earned him an unprecedented five Navy Crosses and an Army Distinguished Service Cross, both the second-highest award for valor (behind only the Medal of Honor) and dozens of other awards, commendations, and medals.

When you choose to boldly persevere, even in the face of difficulty, victory will typically follow. Many times, the greater the risk and difficulty, the greater the reward will be. Sometimes, these rewards are important to just us but many times those acts of perseverance and grit will inspire others. The opposite is also true in that if you give up after the first sign of difficulty and hardships, you will show others this is acceptable. Not everyone is cut out to be a warrior, but with the warriors, risks, and hardship come the spoils and rewards. As Basil King was paraphrased in the 1921 novel *The Conquest of Fear*, "Be bold and mighty forces will come to your aid."

Near the end of WWII, Puller was assigned as commander of the first Marines. Several years later, Lt. Puller led his Marines to a landing at Inchon on September 15, 1950, and eventually his fifth Navy Cross for action during December 5–10 at the Battle of Chosin Reservoir.

About a month after the Chinese got involved in the war, countless Chinese soldiers started to flow south into North Korea to meet the UN forces advancing North. The tide began to turn against the allied troops as they were grossly outnumbered. This was combined with challenging logistics and limited supply lines. Then there was brutal cold weather due to a front from Siberia, plunging temperatures that were thirty-five degrees below zero.

Chesty Puller and his 1st Marines were assigned to help the US Army X Corps break out of the area now known as the Chosen Reservoir. The 30,000 men of the US X Corps found themselves being attacked by over 120,000 Chinese Communist troops. Against overwhelming odds, Marines fought until their last breath. Giving up was never an option for them. The terrain was mountainous, and the cold was unlike anything the UN troops had expected or experienced before in war. The cold not only caused casualty inducing frostbite, but it froze the vehicles and weapons to the point where they could no longer operate. The vicious cold was so debilitating that the Marines at the reservoir said, "It would sink right to your bones." The brutal fighting lasted seventeen days. When the Marines ran out of ammo, they fought hand-to-hand. When their hands were too bloody and frozen to hit the enemy, they used their teeth, rifle butts, and anything else they could do to overcome, adapt, and fight the Chinese onslaught.

"Lead me, follow me, or get the hell out of my way."

—GENERAL GEORGE S. PATTON JR.

Eventually, Chesty's men found themselves surrounded by the twenty-two Chinese divisions, rather than surrendering. Col. Puller calmly answered: "We've been looking for the enemy for several days now. We've finally found them. We're surrounded. That simplifies our problem of finding these people and killing them." His confidence (like his fellow warrior commander, George Patton) inspired others to also not give up. Chesty inspired and led his men by fighting their way out of being surrounded. Chesty's Marines and the soldiers of US Army X Corps inflicted the highest casualty ratio on an enemy in history. They destroyed seven of the twenty-two enemy divisions in the process.

When we become resilient and exhibit the never give up attitude, the way we speak, live, and look at things also changes. Furthermore, our behavior and our relationship with people changes. A significant change happens within us, and the ability to inspire and lead others greatly increases. This attitude is exemplified by the following quote from Chuck Swindoll;

> "The longer I live, the more I realize the impact of attitude on life. Attitude, to me, is more important than facts. It is more important than the past, than education, than money, than circumstances, than failures, than successes, than what other people think or say or

do. It is more important than appearance, giftedness, or skill. It will make or break a company...a church, a home. The remarkable thing is we have a choice every day regarding the attitude we will embrace for that day. We cannot change the inevitable. The only thing we can do is play on the one string we have, and that is our attitude...I am convinced that life is 10 percent what happens to me, and 90 percent how I react to it. And so, it is with you...we are in charge of our attitudes."

Authentic warrior leadership is not just about the individual warrior. It's about inspiring those around you to fight; it's about letting all know that surrender should never be an option. In battle and business, surrendering is always an easy option; it is success that is hard. During the battle, when others lacked the faith to keep fighting, Chesty's leadership told everyone you fight or die. For example, when a frightened Army Major under his command asked about the line of retreat, Chesty radioed his artillery commander and ordered him to fire on any soldier who abandons their position. He then turned back to the stunned Major and said, "That answers your question? There will be no withdrawal."

The "Chesty effect" on the division was apparent as they successfully fought their way out of absolute destruction. A battalion commander recalled, "Puller gave us pride in some way I can't describe. All of us had heard hundreds of stories about him. He kept building up our morale higher and higher, just by being there." As both the bitter cold and overwhelming enemy surrounded the troops, the Marines had to fight their way out against a 360-degree front as they moved south.

You will always have a choice, although the choice may be tough. The option to fight instead of surrendering is usually the tough choice, but it is still a choice. The only way you can truly lose is by choosing to give up. Warriors, entrepreneurs, and the brave people remind us to never retreat, never surrender. In the words of Franklin Roosevelt, "When you find yourself at the end of your rope, tie a knot and hang on."

CHAPTER 13

GRIT

---

*"I love to see a young girl go out and grab the world by the lapels.
Life's a bitch. You've got to go out and kick ass.*

—MAYA ANGELOU

Chesty Puller wasn't just an inspiration for me; he is one of
the most respected and honored Marines in the history of the
Corps. He epitomizes grit. No matter what situation he was
put in, he used his warrior grit to defy all odds and to show
nothing but strength in the face of adversity. One modern
example of Chesty's legacy of grit is Maria Daume. As you
will learn over the next few pages, her grit, resilience, and
bravery had her destined for the Marines.

Maria Daume and her twin brother were born inside a Siberian prison in Russia. In Russia, prisoners were allowed to
keep their babies with them for up to a year in prison. Maria
lived with her mother for that first year in a cold and desolate
Siberian prison. This was the first challenge she faced in her
life. As her mother's first year passed, Maria and her brother
were sent to a Moscow orphanage. Even though she was too

young to remember, that abandonment instilled in her that she would never give up on anything or anyone. At the age of one, she didn't know where or even who her mother (or father) was.

In the Moscow orphanage, Maria looked after her twin brother. At the age of three, she was changing his diapers. Along with all the other girls of the orphanage, she would clean the orphanage and rarely got a chance to enjoy the pleasures of childhood. Within the first five years of her life, Maria experienced challenges most of us could never imagine, but she was a fighter from a young age.

Her life drastically changed for her and her brother when they were adopted by a family from New York.

Her hardships continued even back in the US. Unfortunately, the neighborhood kids were not very welcoming to Maria and her brother. Kids can be very mean to each other, and being a foreigner in a new land sometimes placed a target on Maria and her brother as the bullying began from the kids in her new neighborhood. She was not only an outsider, but she was also an orphan from a far-off, distant land whose accent and difficulty with a new school made things even more challenging. Maria possessed courage and conviction so the bullying didn't bother much, but she couldn't tolerate the abuse her brother was subjected to being a Russian orphan. One of the traits all warriors share is to defend and protect others especially those who can't stand up for themselves. This made Maria a warrior at a very young age—a warrior who had to protect her family and her brother from the world. She stood up to the bullies, and eventually the harassment stopped. Although her grit, tenacity, and courage eventually stopped her schoolmates from bullying them, another battle lay in wait.

Maria's father's chronic abuse of alcohol started to spin out of control. The abuse of alcohol eventually escalated to abuse of drugs. Consequently, her new house, which was her escape and refuge from the orphanage, eventually became even more dysfunctional than the Russian orphanage. Her father's abuse started to escalate. Although the bulling subsided, school was still rough, and things weren't much better at home. Even at a very young age, her warrior shoulders carried a burden that would crush most of us. She felt it was her responsibility to stand up for everyone who she felt was being wronged and ridiculed. This grit is what kept her going during those dark times. One can only imagine the hardships that this young girl endured while still putting others above herself.

> "Look well into thyself; there is a source of strength which will always spring up if thou wilt always look."
>
> —MARCUS AURELIUS

At the age of thirteen, Maria attended a fundraiser with her school called Relay for Life. There, she was drawn to the very fit and athletic US Marines who were recruiting at this event. Their setup highlighted a pull-up bar contraption. They were looking for future Marines that could show how strong they were by participating in a pull-up challenge. Young Maria walked up to the imposing Marines in their sharp uniforms and declared, "I can do pull-ups!" At first the Marines kind of laughed, until young Maria mounted the pull-up bar and started doing pull-ups. The Marines at first thought it was funny and cute that a young thirteen-year-old girl would try to challenge the Marines, but as Maria continued to do more and more pull-ups, their smirks and laughter quickly turned to amazement. Here was a young thirteen-year-old girl, outcompeting the older male Marine warriors. One of the recruiters, Jonathan Butterfield, asked her to come visit his Smithtown recruiting office the minute she turned seventeen. One warrior can always identify another regardless of their size, age, or even gender.

This encounter changed the way Maria Daume thought of herself. It gave her a sense of pride and also a sense of purpose. For the next seven years she kept that statement from the Marine recruiter in the back of her mind. His motivation kept her staying physically active and playing sports year round. She not only wanted to compete in sports, she wanted to be the best and became a five-time varsity basketball player that went on to be recognized as both an all-state but also an All-American athlete. This drive, determination, and grit made her more than qualified to not only become a Marine but also a Marine Infantryman. There was just one small problem, that females were barred from serving in the Marine Corps infantry. For Maria, this wasn't a problem because at seventeen, Maria had overcome challenges that most people couldn't imagine, there was nothing that would stand in the way of her determination of achieving her goals.

When Marina turned seventeen, she proudly walked into the US Marine Corps recruiting station. She was met by Sgt. Jonathan Orlapp, a Marine recruiter decked out in his modified dress blue uniform, chest full of ribbons and medals placed on his uniform filled out by his large chest that tapered to his small waist giving him the awe-inspiring V-shaped physique. He asked her why she was in his office and Maria stated that she was here to become a Marine infantryman. Sgt. Orlapp kind of laughed and said, females can't be infantrymen. For Maria, this was unacceptable, because she knew she was not only as tough and strong as other boys her age, in many cases she was even stronger and tougher. Maria told them they then had a problem because either she goes into the Marines with a 0311 (infantryman) MOS (military occupational specialty) or she wasn't going in at all! Sgt. Orlapp was impressed with her tenacity and her determination.

The warrior spirit is all about never letting anything stand in the way of you accomplishing your life's mission just like Chesty Puller. It doesn't matter if you are an entrepreneur, warrior, or a young teenage girl trying to take on the entire bureaucracy, stubbornness, and century-old traditions of the Marine Corps. Maria was not going away and eventually Sgt. Orlapp introduced her to his boss Gunnery Sergeant Cosh. After hearing some of the same comments about how females can't be infantrymen, Maria laid down a challenge. She asked for a PT (physical training) contest with the other males that were getting ready to ship off to recruit training. Maria beat *every* single male in pull-ups and finished the three-mile run in the top five out of thirty-five men. Eventually her request moved up the proverbial chain of command and her recruiter, Sgt. Orlapp, called her up and said the historic words of: "I want to be the first to congratulate you as the first female in the history of the US Marine Corps to ever receive a contract for the infantry!" Even though she accomplished this incredible achievement, her battle was just starting.

> ## "The greatest pleasure in life is doing what people say you cannot do."
>
> —WALTER BAGEHOT

The experience of making it through recruit training at Parris Island is incredibly difficult on its own, but for Maria it was even tougher. Everywhere her platoon went, they were followed by photographers and journalists. One of the worst things that can happen to a recruit at Parris Island is getting attention. Maria had to endure the jeers from her fellow recruits and the additional hazing from the drill instructors. Nevertheless, she completed initial recruit training at Parris Island in her all-female platoon.

As bad as the drill instructor's harassment was at Parris Island, it was nothing compared to what was waiting for her at one of the world's most difficult and challenging schools: Marine Infantry School. Maria was repeatedly reminded that the place she was fighting for would never belong to her. Infantry was a man's world, and her fellow grunts (Marine infantrymen) were determined to show her she couldn't keep up with them. She always knew that her gender was a barrier in getting to the position that she aimed to reach. However, she wasn't buying any of that, this chauvinism would not stand between her and her goals. Despite consistent pressure, hazing and harassment to quit, she never did. After all, Maria just looked at these as more challenges to overcome. One of those challenges came from holding the eighty-plus pound Mark-19 automatic grenade launcher over your head for as long as you can. All her fellow grunts lined up to undertake this challenge. Maria specifically moved to the back of the line so she could make sure could see who succeeded and who failed at holding this heavy weapon above their head. As she held the eighty-pound weapon above her head almost longer than any of the males, she looked at each of her fellow Marines in her platoon with the same determination and grit that had carried her this far in her life. She showed the platoon she could not only do what the males were doing, she could, in some cases, do even better. She made it clear she deserved to be there just like the rest of the platoon.

After all her initial training she received her orders to report to her first active-duty Marine Infantry units 2/4 in Camp Pendleton, California. As she reported, it was made very clear to her that she was not welcome as this unit did not want a female serving in their ranks. Every day for the first nine month she was harassed unlike anything she could imagine. She was even told by one of her senior Sergeants that he was going to break her, literally. Her fellow Marines did everything they could to make her life miserable. She was depressed, angry, and demotivated. She could feel herself falling into the dark abyss of self-pity that usually ends with giving up. Maria stated, "I was at a point I just didn't care anymore. It was trying on me, I was demotivated, I hated my life. Just because of my anatomy I'm getting hazed, like. Like, I was gone."

Maria understood the sun would rise and the next day might be better. She knew life couldn't always be bad and that it was problematic; there are always good chapters to experience. She not only waited patiently through those tough chapters, she showed all of them her grit and conviction by simply never giving up. It was simple. She couldn't stop time or the natural course of her biology. She couldn't control what was happening to her, but she could control how she reacted to it. She was ready to do whatever it took to get to the next level and earn the respect of her fellow Marines. Everyone around Maria noticed her resilience as she continued to fight back each challenge after challenge.

This was her bottom, her personal abyss, and all these emotions came to a head sitting in a bathroom by herself. Her tears were interrupted by a video call from her mom. Her mom shared that she was giving a presentation about overcoming adversity and used Maria's Marine Corps experience as an example. Two young ten-year-old girls stood up and said, "If Maria can do it, any woman can do it!" Maria snapped out of her self-pity and with tears in her eyes, made the decision to crawl out of the abyss. She was going to show that she was a true warrior just like all the Marines who came before her. Eventually, people who once doubted her began trusting her. They started to recognize her potential. They saw there was no stopping her. She became impossible to break. Eventually the hazing turned to inclusion, and that inclusion turned to respect. Maria's impossible-to-break attitude and warrior spirit eventually allowed her to receive the greatest gift from her fellow Marines: the nickname Daumeinator!

USMC Infantry Mortarman Maria Daume,
"THE DAUMENATOR"

Being in the Marines is an exceptionally tough job. Maria
managed to make her mark within it despite being discrim-
inated against because of her gender and facing ten times
the worse circumstances. Today, Maria is in The National
Museum of the Marine Corps in Quantico with her boots
displayed right up with some of the legends from the Marines
like Chesty Puller himself. The lesson from Maria's story is
simple, but the journey that makes this message available to
us isn't simple at all. There will be times when life will throw
you situations that will try you to your core. There will be
times when things will turn upside down right before your

eyes and you find yourself falling into that abyss. During these times, it will be your grit that will allow you to look at those stressful challenges as opportunities for growth. Steel your nerves and whatever you do, never give up!

The idea of not giving up isn't something new to the world of entrepreneurs. But unfortunately, it is something not many people take very seriously when they jump into the world of entrepreneurship. It is of utmost importance we keep our attitude in line with the never give up mantra if we want to succeed. For example, take Elon Musk. Today, he is considered a game changer in entrepreneurship, but this wasn't always the case. He has suffered his share of setbacks and failures, which he overcame without giving up. That's how he got to the point where he is today.

In 1995, Elon Musk applied for a job at Netscape and failed. In 1996, he was ousted as the CEO of his own company called Zip2, followed by the 1999 crisis, where his PayPal product was considered one of the worst business ideas. In 1999, he crashed one of his most prized possessions, a newly bought McLaren F1 worth a million dollars back then. In 2000, he was ousted from PayPal, and in the same year, almost lost his life to cerebral malaria.

In the next couple of years, Musk kept receiving rejections for all his submissions. He had some successful years after that. In 2008, when the recession hit the world, it hit Musk hard as well. He was on the verge of bankruptcy. There were several other failures, but this man kept failing forward, and today, his net worth stands at almost $183 billion. However, my favorite accomplishment of Musk was watching his face as the SpaceX rocket landed perfectly on the recovery pad ready to be returned to flight just a few weeks later. This incredible accomplishment was the result of decades of hard work and the warrior spirit of never giving up and mission accomplishment even after many rockets before this one crashed and exploded.

The day I began working on my entrepreneurial venture, I made a commitment to myself to not to use the nine-month salary I had been given as a settlement from my former job as a pharmaceutical executive at Eli Lilly and Co. These were supposed to be my savings that would carry our family before my company was profitable enough for me to start drawing a salary. When I started my journey as an entrepreneur, my sales were booming. Everything was going according to plan, and extra financing wasn't quite needed as sales were both small and steady, allowing me to financially support the delay between paying for raw materials and waiting to get paid for goods sold. However, I had no idea how difficult it would be to cover that delay between paying for raw materials and waiting to be paid. My team and I attended the country's largest firefighting trade show, FDIC in Indianapolis. Even though our booth was made from modest materials like a soccer tent with sidewalls held together with zip ties and duct tape, each day our booth traffic increased by the hour. Matter of fact the other nearby booths of well-established multi-million-dollar companies were thanking us for having such long lines that allowed them to exhibit to the people waiting in our line! In just three days, we took orders for almost $100,000 of product. This was a complete shock as my cumulative sales over the previous six months totaled about $5,000. I was completely out of money to fulfill those orders, but I knew I had to find a way. No bank would lend me money as we were new, so I knew the only option was to use my own personal capital and assets I was planning on using as my family's "nest egg."

To cater to these sales, and to produce these materials, I needed enough raw material. However, the business didn't have the finances to purchase that much raw material. Begrudgingly, I tapped into the nine-month salary severance I promised myself I wouldn't use.

That nine-month salary was still not enough to fulfill those orders. Being an ardent wine collector, I had approximately 3,500 bottles of wines that my wife and I collected from Napa and Sonoma, California, where my grandparents lived. I had to let go of those rare and valuable wines so I could convert them to capital for my booming business. There was no way I could have given up and not fulfilled those orders. It was incredibly hard because I held all those bottles close to my heart. They were collected personally and served as a connection to my grandparents and my roots.

However, as more sales started to come in, I needed more cash to keep my venture going. When all of this money wasn't enough, I maxed out all my credit cards. When that stopped working as a solution, I tapped into my 401(K) and took necessary loans out of it. And then, when even that wasn't enough, I ended up mortgaging my house again.

The point is that giving up is the easier option, but it is also the option that stunts your growth as an individual and as a professional. The world is competitive, brutal, and unfair.

When you are out there doing business, the competition is cutthroat. If you don't sustain yourself, if you don't relentlessly strive to accomplish your mission by giving it your all, you will probably never be a successful entrepreneur. You must remember that the *only way that an entrepreneur can fail is if they give up*. Every challenge that comes your way can be tackled, provided you have the faith, tenacity, and warrior spirit to tackle it. This is the grit we need to emulate from all the warriors who never gave up.

Warriors like Chesty Puller and Maria Daume should be our inspirations in never giving up. We will encounter problems at every tangent, on every scale, and at every point in our life. If we start giving up on every situation that makes us a little uncomfortable, we can't quite achieve our life's potential. Each problem has a solution; you just have to be willing to find those solutions, no matter how tough they can be.

Never giving up means you have to solve the problem that put you in the place that makes you want to give up. The unfortunate reality of today is that if you have never been challenged you can become demotivated relatively easily. One of the reasons entrepreneurship is so difficult is that problems often seem overwhelming, and many people without the warrior spirit would give up when faced with those problems. For a warrior to complete their mission and for an entrepreneur to be successful, you must always fight through those problems. Giving up is easy, success is the hard part.

In the Marine Corps, there is one thing that is repeated and practically drilled in the minds of Marines—it is the core value of the warrior mindset. It is that Mission

Accomplishment is number one, and Troop Welfare is number two. The warrior mindset encourages us to look beyond our personal limitations and work toward achieving the peak of our potential.

Take that risk, solve your problems, and become the person who never gives up. As the great football coach Vince Lombardy once said, *"It's not whether you get knocked down; it's whether you get up."*

CHAPTER 14

SACRIFICE

"You have to fight to reach your dream. You have to sacrifice and work hard for it."

—LIONEL MESSI

PART 1

Although many of us actually look at sacrifice as something to be avoided and feared, sacrifice can actually be a beautiful and rare gift. It gives perspective, it allows you to prioritize, it builds discipline. Sometimes the most important things in the warrior's journey are the most difficult. Discipline is the glue that holds the benefits of sacrifice together. Discipline keeps the focus on completing those important tasks no matter how much sacrifice is needed to achieve victory.

It has been said that success equals sacrifice. Although that is not always the case, many times people only see success, but rarely do they see the sacrifices fought behind the scenes. Those who have not embraced the warrior mindset will sometimes take the "easy path" even though the path of adversity and sacrifice is not only the right path, but it is almost always the path that makes you grow.

The ability to embrace sacrifice is critical for entrepreneurs and warriors alike. No warrior can walk into the battlefield without the ability to sacrifice. He walks in knowing he might have to sacrifice his life or see his brothers sacrifice theirs. It is in that sacrifice that a warrior both grows and accomplishes their mission.

The same must be the case with entrepreneurs when they start their businesses. An entrepreneur's journey means everything to them. It is their own child who they have created, nurtured, protected and grown. They need to know that the venture will probably make them sacrifice much more than their friends and acquaintances who work in the traditional workplace. They are willing to give up the safety of the floor so that their ceiling has no limits.

Before we get into the specifics of how sacrifice helps people create, run, sustain, and grow businesses, let us look at the principle of sacrifice. Let's explore a physical example of sacrifice that is the cornerstone of the Polynesian culture. High Chief Sielu Avea from Samoa wears the physical examples of his sacrifice in the ornate and powerful tattoos that cover most of his body. It set him on a journey of determination knowing that his sacrifice made him virtually unbreakable.

The Samoan warrior learns to embrace the sacrifice of physical pain and isolation as he earns his place on the Chief's council.

The Samoan process of tattooing virtually the entire body has been around for centuries. It is a life-threatening physical journey intended to show chiefs that they can withstand the mental and physical pain of this difficult and long ceremonial journey. The yearlong process causes daily sessions where blood flows from the torn flesh caused by the repeated strikes of the mallet onto the sharpened boar's tooth comb that rips apart the flesh inch by inch. The Tufuga Ta Tatau (Samoan master tattooist) hammers the burnt coconut ash into the flesh leaving behind the permanent traditional symbols, images, and artwork. The pain intensifies as more black ash is hammered into the skin over and over again. Only those brave warriors who sacrifice and endure through this dangerous and painful journey of traditional Samoan tattoo will ever be able to participate in the High Chief's council.

This is the crucible all Samoan chiefs need to face.

While today most of us don't get a life-threatening full-body tattoo that may kill us, we are all, at some point, asked to make sacrifices. The sacrifices we make end up being the words on the pages of our life's novel. Many times, the sacrifices we avoid may bring temporary reprieve, they also deprive us of the opportunity for growth. It is at the crucible that those sacrifices prepare you to prevail. To make it through those difficult crucibles, warriors realize they have to transform to succeed.

Once the traditional Samoan tatau (tattoo) ceremony is started, it has to be finished. That does not mean the Tufuga Ta Tatau has to finish the tatau in one sitting. In fact, the painful and dangerous process is almost always separated into many sessions to give the warrior's body time to heal before they continue to the next part of their body. However, the tatau has to be finished at all costs. A person whose tatau wasn't finished will bear the mark of cowardice, pala'ai, and bring shame to himself and his family.

Females also endure the sacrifice of tatau, but the female tatau was traditionally reserved for the high chief's daughter, the taupou, who was responsible for dancing the siva (Samoan dance) and mixing 'ava (ground drink from root vegetable) at special occasions.

High Chief Sielu Avea grew up on the Polynesian island of Samoa. In 1980, he left his island home to move to Hawaii after receiving a scholarship at BYU in Honolulu, Hawaii. After his graduation, Chief Seilu worked at the Polynesian culture center near Oahu's north shore for over twenty years. He was initially looking for a better way to take care of his two kids and wife. One of his first jobs was in the hotel industry putting on a traditional luau.

My family and I first met Chief Seielu on one of our annual trips to Hawaii. We were immediately taken in by his warm smile and tattoos that completely covered his body from his knees to his chest. Visiting with him and seeing his fellow Samoan warrior participate in his Fia Fia Luau is always one of the highlights of our trip to this island paradise.

High Chief Sielu Avea (left) and author's young son Bryce Green (right), Ko Olina Resort, Oahu, Hawaii

Chief Seilu honors the people who come to his luau by celebrating this island paradise and bring back his message of love, hope, and joy to the mainland. They come to the islands of Hawaii to soak in the raw Polynesian beauty and healing "Aloha Spirit." Some come to celebrate, and some come to heal from bad experiences back home. The luau is a traditional feast combined with entertainment. It transforms all who attend to a place of Polynesian paradise where, just for a few hours, the attendees can leave behind their past and soak up the culture, love and energy of the Polynesian people. It was the dream of Chief Seilu to have to share the love and happiness of the Polynesian people to all those who visit Hawaii and attend his luau. He named it "Fia Fia," which roughly translates to "the happy celebration."

> "Every wish, every dream, every idea comes to existence only through blood, sweat and sacrifice."
>
> —IVAN MOODY

As is the case for many entrepreneurs, it was incredibly tough for him in the beginning. The large crowds rarely showed and as a result his income wasn't in line with his expectations. The only plus that kept him going was that every week the crowd would grow a little bit more than the previous week. He had to sacrifice his time with his family as he put his heart and soul into marketing and promoting his luau. It was a slow transition, but it was happening. Slowly, the audience grew and grew from sixteen to 400 to 700. Eventually, they literally had to have a waiting list. Those early sacrifices and hardships started to pay off.

"A river cuts through rock, not because of its power, but because of its persistence."

—JAMES N. WATKINS

Chief Seilu was familiar with sacrifice. When he was a young man growing up in the jungle, it was a life of survival off the land. His father had a job at the college, and he would help him out with tasks like mowing the lawn and collecting things at work. The thirty dollars a month wasn't a lot, but it did keep them afloat.

Every Christmas, until Chief Seilu stopped going to high school, his father would give him one dollar. That single dollar meant the world to him. He watched his father work hard, which instilled in him unbreakable motivation and drive. He watched his father help people by getting them work so they could take home food for their families. It was this circle of helping others that were early observations that motivated his passion of hard work and helping others.

With his father as his primary inspiration, a young Chief Seilu and his family moved to the village to be closer to his elders. He continued his family's and culture's tradition by helping his elders. Cooking for them and keeping them company were new experiences.

In the village, Chief Seilu also received his education, which was different than what the other children in town experienced. Unlike other kids his age, he sacrificed the joys of youth as his father's strict rules forbade him from dating and hanging out with his friends. His father wanted him to avoid those distractions as he absorbed his family's culture and lived off the land. Dances, parties, and games were replaced with learning survival skills like fishing, cooking, building a house, and more.

When kids in the nearby towns were attending their high school prom, Chief Seilu was learning traditional lessons from his elders. He listened to their interesting stories and funny anecdotes. He absorbed a lot of wisdom from the time he spent with the elders. They always gave him their blessings as they taught him to grow, give, respect, love, and share.

In a way, this traditional way of growing up was a sacrifice that Chief Seilu was making. He gave up the care-free teenage life to pursue a simpler life, which taught him valuable lessons and prepared him for life's difficult challenges that lay ahead. His father's hard work ethic and his compassion for others were lifelong lessons emulated by him for decades to come. Chief Seilu's job of taking care of horses that were used for transportation gave him a firsthand seat to the stories of the elder warrior-like men. In these villages, everybody depended on the oldest male as provider and judge. The oldest male was not only the wisest but also the one who had overcome many obstacles and understood the concept of sacrifice.

Many decades later in Hawaii, the manager of the hotel Chief Seilu worked at came to him and told him they didn't think they could continue the luau contract with him for the next year. The management had changed, and the new management didn't see the value in renewing Chief Seilu's luau contract. He tried to persuade the new management, but they persisted in their decision to cancel his luau he worked so hard to grow. He told the new management he would be back. He would not give up; he recognized this not as an opportunity to accept defeat but rather a way to convince them that the guests needed him as much as he and his performers needed them. There was no anger and no malice, just determination and faith he would once again share his aloha message of happiness through his luau.

In a little less than three months, Chief Seilu was called back by the new management and offered a new contract to continue his luau. He knew the sacrifices he had made over the last several months did not go unnoticed. The fact that so many returning guests asked about Chief Seilu and why his luau wasn't scheduled let the new management know how special his luau was to others. He always had faith in himself, but the fact that so many strangers asked for him let him know that the sacrifice of being unemployed for three months would only make him and his fellow performers appreciate their gift of luau even more. While many others would angrily quit and found a new line of employment, that was not what he learned in his formative years back home in Samoa. Those early sacrifices from his home island of Samoa gave him the warrior's courage and confidence to find a way back no matter how tough those three months were to him, his family, and his employees. All of what happened in his early life made him the man he is today. So many experiences from his earlier life are great lessons to the warrior in all of us.

Growing up in the Polynesian islands was not as glamorous as big city life in the mainland but he was surrounded by happiness, love, respect for his elders and the beauty of the Pacific. It was the tropical beauty of his surroundings and the compassion of his fellow islanders that kept him so positive and made him such a determined individual. It was teamwork, faith, hard work, and the sanctity of the tribes in the village that made everyone content with their lives. This upbringing and positive attitude are common characteristics of successful entrepreneurs and warriors alike. He has spent his entire life following the principles of a warrior.

"Pain is weakness leaving the body."

—TOM SOBAL

Now, let us dig into the transformation Chief Seilu experienced: Chief Seilu's tattoos that made him the man he is today. The tattoo ceremony and the permanent Polynesian spiritual designs are both literally and figurative physical sacrifices.

Growing up and watching people get the tattoo, he never wanted to have to experience that physical and mental pain. He had seen how much they hurt. Many people die because these tattoos get infected, or they end up with big wounds on their bodies that never fully heal. However, as he grew older and started learning things about leadership and how everything around the village elders lead, he found that getting tattooed was a very important part of his culture.

For him, culture was a significant part of who he was and who he wanted to be.

When he was called to attend council by the head of state, the first thing Chief Seilu told him was that he wanted him to have a say. The head of state just kind of smiled at the young Chief Seilu. That smile hid behind him knowing how a young warrior would be treated by the elders if he spoke up without proving his place in the council through both the sacrifice and experience of the tattoo ceremony. Chief Seilu finally realized he was strong and almost swaggered into the first council meeting of the chiefs. He waited for his time to speak and when he stood up to talk, he was quickly shouted down by the elders. They told him he was not "covered in the proper attire." Until he had proven himself by becoming covered in the traditional tattoo and yearlong associated ceremony, he was not welcome to address the others who had already proven their determination and sacrifice. In formal tribal council meetings, one's wisdom, power, and influence are determined not by the attire of their body being covered in traditional tattoo but rather the sacrifice it represents.

Today, we see many people get tattoos. Some even get them every month and cover their entire bodies. However, people get these tattoos in safe environments and under the guidance of medical and governmental regulations. In the traditional tattoo ceremony in Samoa, tattoos are done in the traditional style with sharpened whale bones and wild boar tusks. They are colored by the deep black pigment made from the ashes of coconuts. When chiefs get tattoos, it isn't just about the tattoo; it is about the pain that comes with it and how it represents the warrior spirit of growing and learning through sacrificial pain. It is about the sacrifice and determination of spending time by yourself as the yearlong ceremony requires you to remain totally pure—no alcohol, no sexual activity. You spend your days in a thatch hut as you recover from each daily tattoo session. It is about the perspective you gain from a year of not drinking alcohol, seeing your friends, or even having the companionship of your spouse. The pain doesn't just stop with the actual tattoo but also lingers by tolerating and prevailing through the healing process. This healing process is exacerbated by the pain of having to bathe in the ocean after each session as you work the salt water into your open wounds. Many warriors die from infection and exhaustion during this process as a result of the aforementioned hardships.

It is said that all of this helps the chiefs with leadership. It makes them patient and teaches them how to sacrifice when challenges show up. Sacrifice prepares you for the worst that could come your way. The more you learn to deal with sacrifice, the easier your challenges become. Prevailing through sacrifice helps the warrior prepare for any obstacles that stand in the way of their mission.

Chief Seilu Avea worked hard to become a chief. He prevailed through the challenges and made the associated sacrifices less difficult as he focused and learned from the pain. He got to a point where he was asked to almost sacrifice his life to become the Chief, and he did. He is an inspiration as an absolute warrior for all of us. Think of the mental and physical pain Chief Sielu Avea overcame. It is no wonder he has prevailed as both a warrior and entrepreneur. Those early childhood lessons and painful experiences in Samoa prepared him to prevail through the difficult times he encountered as an entrepreneur and founder of one of the most successful luaus in Hawaii.

PART 2

I've learned the importance of sacrificing short-term pleasures for long-term happiness. Life is a long game, and when you start a business, you've made a decision that doesn't allow any time in year one to focus on anything but building it. I'm talking code red, 18-hours-a-day dedicated—even at the mercy of your family time. But in two or three years, when I'm taking my kids on business trips and showing them the world, we're reaping the benefits.

—GARY VAYNERCHUK, FOUNDER, AND CEO OF VAYNERMEDIA

Dreams are a significant part of who we are. They make us, or they break us, and the only difference between the two situations is how we put our effort into it. People around the world choose to be warriors, in the most literal sense of the word, and when they make that decision, they know they have put everything on the line to be sacrificed in the name of their passion, vigor, and self-belief. The same logic and understanding apply to entrepreneurs because they know they are warriors in their own field.

The term sacrifice is used commonly. However, the real brunt of the word is faced by people who risk everything to attain that one goal that they have set for themselves. For warriors, that goal could be a victory for their tribe, country, or any piece of land they are fighting for. On the other hand, for entrepreneurs, that goal is attaining a certain stature in their field, making a difference in society or making a certain amount of money for themselves and their investors.

As fortunate and unfair as life could be, the attainment of goals, regardless of your field or profession, success is dependent on how much you are willing to give. Sometimes, what is required of us stops many people from being their best self and fulfilling their destiny. However, there are times when the pain of sacrifice is worth the price of success. This sacrifice could subject you and your family to extreme emotional duress. For example, you need more cash flow than your sales and creditors can provide. As a result, sometimes personal sacrifices need to be made to fill the gap that the lack of cash presents. You might have to sell something dear to you, you may have to risk personal assets and treasures. It could be your house, your car, your jewelry.

Let's look at some other sacrifices that an entrepreneur is expected to make as they ride the proverbial entrepreneurial roller coaster.

STABILITY

When you're starting a new venture, it is not guaranteed you will succeed. Matter of fact a failed start-up can cause the founder significant hardship such as bankruptcy, loss of friends, difficulty in finding future employment and diminished health. No matter how solid your business plan is structured, no matter how great your team, at the end of the day the odds show many more start-ups fail rather than succeed. You must be ready to sacrifice comfort or stability when you venture into murky waters of a start-up business. Stability takes time. Setbacks happen, mistakes become learning opportunities and you must possess unbreakable fortitude to survive the early years. Your venture is like your baby, which will take time to grow. A baby has to fall down many times before they can walk. The same is true for entrepreneurs.

WORK AND LIFE BALANCE

When you're working for someone else, you typically focus on your job at work. It is easy to leave behind the stress and challenges of your day's work when you are back at home with your friends and family. However, that starts to change when you venture into your own business. There are no fixed hours, and the lines between your work and private life begin to blur. This is because work life becomes private life. Vacations may help you experience nice resorts and unique places, but your phone is always on and the fear of missing an important email usually takes priority to a relaxing walk on the beach or focused time being present with family and friends. Balance can be ellusive for the entrepreneur. One also needs to be realistic and know that there is only so much a person can handle. Being ready to sacrifice certain aspects of your personal life and health can be a perfect recipe to drastically and unexpectedly bring an abrupt halt to your entrepreneurial dreams. Warriors sacrifice their personal lives and spaces all the time, but it is important that sacrifice is balanced and weighed against the price of success.

My wife and I couldn't afford to pay rent, so we decided that she will stay at her sister's while I stayed at my mother's. We didn't leave each other; we just lived apart until I got back on my feet. Recently, my son (now twenty-five) confronted me about leaving them for a year. I explained that it was necessary to build the business and give him the life he deserved. My son works with me today and is reaping the rewards. It wasn't an easy pill to swallow at the time, but I knew the sacrifice would eventually be worth it. Today, money isn't a problem. And it's because I did what had to be done to build my dream.

—JOHN HANNA, THE AUTHOR OF WAY OF THE
WEALTHY AND CEO OF FAIRCHILD GROUP

HEALTH

Another sacrifice you might have to make on your entrepreneurial journey could be your health. This isn't a sacrifice you should willfully make. However, sometimes, this is a sacrifice that ends up being made without realizing that the warrior's relentless drive clouds their ability to be physically and mentally healthy. Be ready to miss birthdays, anniversaries, and New Year's parties when you embark on this journey, but the warrior can never appreciate the fruits of their labor if their health is sacrificed.

FINANCES

When you embark on the quest for more money typically associated with owning your business you also sacrifice financial stability. The stability the average salary brings is usually replaced by uncertainty of a larger income. In the early days of your business, there is a significantly high chance you will not have the best of earnings or in some cases *any* income. One needs to be prepared for a sacrifice in their lifestyle because of the uncertainty of recurring income. As a result, the personal savings of your previous income and setting aside money in a "rainy day fund" is critical to weather the lows that entrepreneurial financial uncertainty brings. I can speak firsthand of how important it is in the early days to prepare for the uncertainty of the impending storm.

SLEEP

We hear all about how sleep is essential for our body, our mind, and our overall health. While I agree with that, let me break this to you: Sleep is a concept alien to newly venturing entrepreneurs. You will have to sacrifice sleep, as well. Some of this will be because you have errands to run very early in the morning or a little late in the night, and sometimes it might just be stress and trying to keep a work-life balance. This might sound like a small sacrifice to make, but sleep deprivation can result in many unexpected repercussions.

Be aware of the unavoidable challenges lack of eight hours of sleep brings. Investigate mindfulness skills such as power naps, meditation, and other stress relieving activities.

COMFORT

When you start your own company, it means you will have to do many jobs that might have been delegated to other people when you were working for someone else. There will be tough decisions you would need to make and tasks you will perform that may seem "beneath" you.

Doing multiple and menial tasks pushes you out of your comfort zone. Sacrificing your comfort and your bubble is one of the most significant and unexpectant impacts of becoming an entrepreneur. The most successful entrepreneurs are the ones who approach uncomfortable situations with confidence, as they thrive on finding their comfort in the most uncomfortable places.

"Entrepreneurship is living a few years of your life like most people won't, so that you can spend the rest of your life like most people can't."

—ANONYMOUS

CHAPTER 15

MORALITY

Over the previous pages, we have shared examples around warrior attributes ranging from purpose to courage to grit. However, there is one trait that is the glue that holds all the warrior traits together: morals. Without integrity and a set of morals, the warrior would be nothing other than a rudderless ship. There is a code that all warriors have. Although that moral code could range from culture to culture and it adjusts from time to time, it always has to be the North Star that warriors follow. For some, the North Star could be as straightforward as following the ten commandments, for others it could be the Geneva Convention or UCMJ (Uniform Code of Military Justice). Sometimes, the line between law and morals does not always line up. It is this "grey" area that the morals of the warrior will need to guide their actions. Without following a moral code, a warrior will be nothing more than a criminal.

Let's unpack this concept of the grey area. For many individuals their moral code may be that you should never lie, cheat, or steal. For others, those actions may be necessary for them to accomplish their mission. What happens when the only way you can accomplish your mission is to deceive, lie and spy on potential adversaries. That is exactly the case when it comes to espionage, a profession that can be traced back to a spy in the court of King Hammurabi around 1750 BC. Espionage, deception and subversion are all critical tools on both the battlefield as in the boardroom. For example, Thomas Aquinas thought all lies were wrong, but he also taught that there was a hierarchy in which some lies were necessary and even advantages and so were pardonable. Entrepreneurs have to venture into that grey area when they may need a strategy to confuse or fight their competition. Nevertheless, when venturing into this "grey" area it is even more important to have your moral compass not allow you trespass into that area that violates both your personal and organization's moral boundary. Let's look at a real-life story from my friend, my friend who we will just call, Jeff. Jeff was in the CIA and was like a modern day "Q" from the James Bond movies. Jeff never thought he would be a CIA spy but through a series of chances and meeting the right people at the right time, he found himself being recruited in to one of our nation's premiere warrior agencies. Jeff prevailed in his time in the agency as he mastered the craft of surveillance, deception, and subversion.

Jeff's experiences in the CIA highlighted how ethics are extremely situationally subjective. Many have said it is impossible to be an ethical warrior because they may have to violate one of the most significant commandments that says, "Thou shall not kill." Others can look at that same commandment and interpret it as, "Thou shall not murder." All murders are killers but not necessarily are all killers murderers. It is possible to kill another in self-defense or kill a cow for food and not violate the morals laid out in the ten commandments. The same is true in business. What happens if one business uses deception to make a competitor think they are bigger and stronger than they actually are so that competitor doesn't feel like they could take advantage of them? These moral "grey areas" are the intersection between doing anything to complete your mission and at the same time not violating your personal moral code. As the old saying goes, "War is hell," and so is starting a business. In war, many times you will be forced between the very fine line of what is needed to accomplish your mission and what may be morally sound. Always be aware of that line as sometimes accomplishing the mission may not be worth compromising both your and society's moral standards. Be careful as you venture into that area, as many times it is very hard to go back once you compromise your integrity.

For normal people and citizens, the morality of deception, killing, and subversion is very black and white. However, that black and white starts to become grey as a warrior or law enforcement agencies may have to lie to keep their cover or listen to a message that wasn't intended for them. What would you do if you were accidentally sent an email detailing your competitors' presentation for a highly competitive bid? Would you look at it? Would you notify the competitor? Would you adjust your strategy if the competitors' presentation exposed their "blind spots"?

Now, spying is also something that may violate normal moralistic codes, but what about if it is done for national security? This was a daily situation Jeff had to navigate during his time with the CIA. Jeff learned this early on in his training as he was taught traits to deceive our enemy such as training at undisclosed facilities where they would cover their license plates, so the Soviet satellites were kept in the dark.

One of the instances he vividly remembers in particular was a mock dinner party where Jeff and his fellow trainees were supposed to analyze people around them and then report back without being noticed. One of the lessons he learned from that exercise was the importance of working together as a team so that others could coordinate surveillance so as not to expose any one individual. Imagine how easy it would be to be noticed if you never left the side of someone at a small party. Now imagine how easy it would be if you worked as a team to spread out the surveillance and secretly communicate to ensure the subject was never by themselves and several people came and went throughout the evening so as to not have them notice any one individual for too long. The CIA officers were taught very early on that many times a team is needed to accomplish your mission. If you don't have good people surrounding you and working together to achieve a common goal, it can be very difficult to be a successful warrior or an entrepreneur.

This is something that has been reiterated throughout the book as well. Remember, just as an engine needs all its parts in good working order to function, a team needs its every member to be on the same line. Even if a single person from the team doesn't follow what has been planned, things can go haywire. For example, if in the middle of the battle, one individual warrior falls asleep on guard duty allowing the enemy to sneak into their sector. That small mistake could not only compromise a battle but lose an entire war. Imagine if you were the one in the aforementioned scenario that accidentally clicked "reply all" instead of "reply" when you sent your presentation in advance of a meeting to all of your competitors and the customer and not just the customer.

Let's get back to Jeff and his story. Jeff and his team were traveling across the globe on a secret mission. It is typical they always had to coordinate with the logistics team as they had to transport equipment in with them. Sometimes, those logistic officers even had to share lodging with them. Treating the logistic team as members of the team was essential as no matter how significant your role is, you are all on the same team. No individual is a big or small part of a team, they all have a job to do, and it doesn't matter if a big or small part fails, all the parts need to be treated with equal respect. Remember the space shuttle Columbia exploded all because a small rubber O-ring failed. That piece of equipment that probably cost a few cents was just as important as one of the million-dollar-plus rocket motors.

Everyone matters. Every single thing matters, be it a receptionist, an intern, or the CEO himself—all of them have an essential role to play in the functioning of a business or anything else. If the team succeeds, then you succeed. And, if you play your role properly and succeed, then the team succeeds as well. It is a two-way street here for everyone involved. There is always so much more one can achieve if they work as a team.

During his time in the CIA, Jeff always made it a point to show up early. He made sure that he was the first one to arrive because not only did he want to do his job right, but he also wanted to be there for anything that might or might not go wrong. He would volunteer for holiday duty and work Christmas and New Year's. He always put the team above himself. According to Jeff, "If you're there, you are going to be tackling problems head on and getting more experience by just being present. Regardless of the outcome, if you just show up and keep trying, you will come to realize that failure is not necessarily something permanent. If you can adapt and not lose sight of what the ultimate objective is, everything will be alright. Failure is nothing but a lesson for the future."

One example of failure and then learning we can take from Jeff's life is the incident where they were building a multimillion-dollar piece of equipment. Everything was going to plan; it was crated and packaged. However, when they started to uncrate it, the circuit boards on the inside were knocked off. It was at this point that they realized that during shipping they had planned for a ramp but when they arrived there was no ramp but rather a six-foot drop off at the back of C-141. That drop knocked off the circuit board and severely hampered that mission. At the time, this logistical failure was debilitating. However, during their after-action debriefing, they were able to use this failure as a learning point that updated their doctrine and helped many future missions.

Entrepreneurs, too, need to learn from their failures because without the failures we can never appreciate success. The road of the warrior is filled with detours, dead ends, and dangers. No failure is permanent and everything you encounter on your journey is an opportunity for growth and learning even though there may feel like there is no tomorrow.

"By seeking and blundering we learn."

—JOHANN WOLFGANG VON GOETHE

IT'S NOT ALWAYS ABOUT MONEY

"Giving does not just feel good, but it's really, really good for business, and it's good for your personal brand."

—BLAKE MYCOSKIE

For many entrepreneurs, success can be measured not in dollars but in how they help others. Many people think of money as a scorecard while others think of money as a conduit to helping to make the world a better place. One of those people is Blake Mycoskie. Blake's business model does not look at money as a scorecard but rather how many people he can help as his scorecard. His business model is predicated on the concept where every time one of his customers purchases one pair of shoes from his company, he will donate one to the poverty-driven countries in Africa and Asia. He advocates for global poverty and raises awareness for health problems in the third world.

This concept originated while he was on vacation in Argentina in 2006. It was there that his life changed and his mission of giving back became clear. He always knew at the back of his mind that children in poverty-driven countries travel without shoes, but this was the first time he saw the sores, the scars, and the blisters with his own eyes. It had a profound effect on him, and he joined a volunteer organization that also wanted to help with this problem. With them, he went village to village distributing shoes to the children in need. That gave him the idea for the one-for-one business model in which they donated a shoe for everyone a customer bought. That concept became the basis for his company, TOMS. His company has now helped over one hundred million lives and has now progressed from providing shoes to the needy to optical treatments, prescription glasses, surgeries, clean drinking water, and children's books to those in need.

Not only has he helped and given shoes to millions of people, but he has also helped thousands recover from losing sight. Your morals are the guiding light to your why. Be it defending your country or donating to those in need, make sure you never compromise your morals on your journey.

CHAPTER 16

SERENITY

———

It's very difficult to be successful and happy in any job if you don't take care of your mental health. Without serenity, it is very difficult to achieve true success. What is the purpose of accomplishing your mission if you can't enjoy the spoils? Mental health is a taboo for most warriors and even entrepreneurs. Acknowledgment of the dark subject of mental health is finally getting the attention it deserves, but we still have a long way to go.

Our nation's premier law enforcement agency is the Federal Bureau of Investigation. They are notorious for their professionalism, integrity, and law enforcement excellence. However, these brave special agents and FBI employees are still humans. They have families and personal lives that need to be balanced with an immense amount of pressure and stress that comes from seeing the aftermath of some of the most violent crimes. Couple this with long hours and physical and mental stress, and it can be a recipe for tragedy. The following story is of an FBI agent who worked through that mental pressure and ensured there was serenity in his life.

FBI Executive Assistant Director, Intelligence, Eric

Let's call this FBI agent Eric to make things simpler. Eric got involved with the bureau when he was only nineteen years old. It all began for him in the FBI's Puerto Rico office in San Juan. His first exposure to those who wish to do harm to the

US was when he witnessed a rocket attack by a terrorist group on the San Juan Field office. As a result, the FBI concluded there needed to be increased security at night to both deter and look out for future attacks. His father, at that time, was in the FBI and recommended he apply for this entry-level position.

It seemed like a rather lucrative offer because it was not only well paid, but it also gave you the opportunity to be part of the FBI. That entry-level job catapulted Eric to rise all the way up to the rank of Executive Assistant Director in the FBI.

The first day on the job there was a big gang arrest. As the gang members were being processed in the field office, Eric saw the perpetrators flanked by heavily armed FBI tactical agents in full tactical gear. Just seeing those agents process these hardened criminals lit a fire in him that would take him to some of the highest positions in the FBI over the next few decades.

Eric, extremely enthusiastic about his future, completed high school, later college, and then joined the FBI Academy. At the time, the war on drugs was a significant part of the FBI's focus. The southwest border was a critical station, and agents fluent in Spanish were needed. Eric enthusiastically volunteered for this important assignment of actively working drug cases.

Eric worked several cases in which they confiscated over 2,000 pounds of marijuana, along with some one hundred-plus kilos of cocaine. He regularly investigated major cartels along with some of the most violent criminals in the world. In one case Eric had to balance the stress of bringing the Mexican cartels to justice at the same time his wife gave birth to his son. On top of all of that hurricane George destroyed the house they were building for their new family.

It cannot be stressed enough that any one of these events would be almost too much for someone to handle but warriors are trained to compartmentalize and prioritize. Even though warriors train for the worst things to happen at the worst times, at the end of the day, warriors are still human and need to have coping mechanisms. Without those coping mechanisms that we will go into in more detail toward the end of this chapter, it is very difficult for a warrior to handle that level of stress and pressure.

To make matters worse, when they rebuilt their home that was lost to the hurricane, they later found out that the financing company was involved in a Ponzi scheme, and they lost all of their money rebuilding the new home. He eventually requested transfer to FBI headquarters in Washington, DC, as a supervisor so his family could once again try and have their dream home. With the transfer to FBI HQ, he started the next phase of his career as a supervisor. Even after moving to Washington, DC, he continued to work many narcotic cases involving everything from high-level cartels and major dealers. However, after 9/11 everything changed.

Like many others in the FBI and other federal law enforcement agencies, he was reassigned to a terrorism task force. He recalls it as being an exciting move because he was now directly linked to national security in the post 9/11 posture of the FBI.

Finally, in the year 2016, he retired from the FBI as the Head of the Intelligence Division. His thirty-one-year journey took him from a nighttime security guard to being one of the FBI leaders responsible for our nation's sovereignty. In those thirty-one years, he was a firsthand witness to the evils of some of the most hardened criminals. One case that deeply impacted him was the Runyon case.

In July 2002, Eric was stationed in Orange County, Los Angeles. He was a supervisor in the narcotic division at that time. One of the FBI's specialties is kidnapping and when a kidnapping happens, FBI agents from all divisions will typically be assigned to those cases. This specific case involved a little six-year-old girl named Samantha Runyon who was playing in her front yard and had a man approach her, grab her, and whisk her away. The case was initially being investigated by the Orange County Sheriff's department who requested the help of the FBI and his team.

Part of Eric's responsibility in the early days of the case involved knocking on the neighbors' doors and interviewing them to see if they could provide any leads or clues. Hundreds and thousands of leads started to come in as more and more media covered the case. As the investigation progressed, the family would keep in constant contact with Eric and his team. He became very close with the family and couldn't help putting him in their position as he had a child almost the same age as Samantha.

Eventually, the worst was realized as they found Samantha Runyon's body just off the side of the road dumped into a bush. She had been brutally killed. Even though they all wished for the best, as the days and weeks progressed, they all knew that this was the most probable outcome. Nevertheless, when it happened, it was a brutal shock to all involved. Eric looked at the crime scene images of Samantha Runyon in the bushes, and he couldn't help but make a comparison between her and his own daughter. These precious and innocent girls shared the same long hair and had a striking resemblance. The image of this innocent and beautiful girl brutalized and left in a bush on the side of the road was seared in his head. As more details came out, it was confirmed she had also been sexually assaulted and then strangled as she was left to die in that bush.

The nightmares followed the second guessing of what he and the other officers could have done differently. He couldn't help seeing the face of his own daughter every time he reimagined those horrific crime scene photos.

He could handle seeing adult drug dealers kill each other. He could handle the horrors of the Mexican drug cartels, but the murder of a child was just simply something too much for him to mentally process. He knew the real work was just getting started; he had to catch the monster responsible for this disgusting murder. He had to find the serenity to do his job and at the same time balance the mental toll this case was taking on him.

He pushed through the horrors of this entire incident and did everything in his capacity to find the culprit behind the abduction and murder of this innocent girl. He worked late nights and extra hours to make sure no stone was left unturned in the investigation. After processing thousands of leads sifting through mountains of evidence, the monster who kidnapped and murdered Samantha was arrested. His name was Andrew Aviva from Lake Elsinore, California.

In 2005, the man was found guilty and given the death penalty. As Eric returned to his intelligence work, something wasn't right. He was struggling to get a hand on debilitating restlessness and emotional pain. Although his injuries were not noticeable to his friends and colleagues, inside he was falling apart. He realized he needed help. This was his crucible, and this case brought him too close to that dark abyss. He was changed and he needed help. Eric eventually sought mental health counseling and started the road to recovery. Through the therapy he looked at life differently, he realized how precious life is and how important it was for him to be a great father to his daughter. He fought the warrior stereotype of avoiding help and he prevailed through his crucible.

Even an FBI officer can fall prey to the mental spiral caused from the warrior's battles. It is okay to ask for help when you lose your serenity. The last few pages of this book focus on ways to keep your mental health in balance, but in the cases where that is not enough, *ask for help*. Accomplishing your life's mission is important but if your work isn't bringing you happiness and you are struggling mentally, something is wrong. **A warrior can't be a warrior if they don't take care of themselves.**

All of this doesn't just matter a lot for your happiness, but also for your productivity of work and the level of work that you do. If you are unhappy and your mental capabilities are not supporting you the way they ideally should, then you have found yourself in trouble. You will not be happy, your work will not be up to the standard it needs to be, and everything will fall like dominos, one after the other. To keep it concise, keep your mental health on the top of your priorities because if you don't, it will cripple all your other priorities before you even realize what is happening.

And so, we arrive at the conclusion of our journey together. Throughout the entire book, we have talked about everything that makes a good entrepreneur—a good warrior who takes upon every adversity and every problem by its course. However, in the midst of all of that, what we tend to ignore, and what these warriors and entrepreneurs tend to ignore themselves as well, is the importance of mental health.

Having the attitude of a warrior is exponentially beneficial, but it also comes with its drawbacks, that if not controlled, can lead to bigger and rather negative consequences. One of these includes the deterioration of mental health. Being a warrior or an entrepreneur means that you have to be a go-getter. You need to be the person who absorbs all the stress and all the pressure that comes with the job. Sometimes you need to be the person who works all the time, away from friends, family, and more, which makes you lonely and puts you in an absurd sense of isolation. Most of us, particularly in the COVID-19 pandemic, have felt the after-effects of being in isolation in terms of health, particularly mental health, and the results have been shockingly severe. Let's look at the traits and a few characteristics of a warrior: strong, aggressive, smart, adverse, courageous, decisive, and many more. All of these characteristics, as already discussed in the book in detail, apply to entrepreneurs as well. More than mental health concerns that happen during a certain course of action, for warriors and entrepreneurs, post-traumatic stress disorder, commonly referred to as PTSD, is a serious concern. For a warrior, PTSD might be a result of a being exposed to the horrors of the battlefield. On the other hand, for an entrepreneur, it might be the aftermath of losing an entire business owing to one or two unforeseen circumstances.

SUPPORT FOR WARRIORS

We are all human beings who get affected by our surroundings and the people around us. No matter how strong you are, stress can be as bad as a slow poison for us and our health. A plethora of research has been done on how stress affects our physical and mental health.

People always need other people to lift them and support them to make things happen. Having supportive individuals around you can keep stress at bay as well. This is how human nature works. Human beings are inherently social beings. They need to interact to be able to function correctly, especially in terms of mental health concerns. Since our reference point is warriors, let us look at how vital this emotional and psychological support is for them.

First, we need to understand that warriors, military personnel, and fighters experience a lot of traumatic incidents directly. Most of these individuals tend to store it in their minds and memories and then are troubled forever. Amid this trouble, what they need is support. Times can get dark and difficult for them as they battle through and witness blood, death, pain, and misery.

This kind of stress, even though rather prevalent in military departments, isn't just limited to fighters. Workplaces, especially if you are running them, tend to have similar pressures that draw you into making wrong decisions and playing with your health.

For situations like those, it is essential to have support and a team that stands with you. That team will also ensure to take over in case of your absence. There can't be enough emphasis on the fact that networks are essential to sustain a business, primarily because of how high stress levels in workplaces are today.

Support provided by friends, family, and coworkers reduces the negative effects of stressful situations on physical and emotional well-being (Schaefer et al., 1981).

There is no denying the fact that teamwork and support are integral parts of becoming successful and retaining that success. Entrepreneurs don't just need logistical support during office hours. They also need trustworthy assistance that makes sure their physical and mental health remains stable. This is why physical fitness, adequate sleep, hobbies, and mindfulness are so important to both the warrior and the entrepreneur. This support will make you flourish as a businessperson or a warrior, and also help you be mentally sound, even in times of trouble.

SELF CARE

Either way, the fact remains that even though the statistics proving my point are astoundingly high, the efforts into countering these aren't as high as they should be. If the issues are not taken care of properly, they often lead to worst-case scenarios like suicide, self-harm, and sometimes even other violent acts against people around them. As a result, it would be fair to conclude that while warriors and entrepreneurs need to work hard and attain a certain sense of composure and skillset, they must also ensure their mental well-being is not negatively affected.

To verify these claims, let us first look at some statistics and facts about military and PTSD today and then discuss an entrepreneur who overcame mental health issues to become successful and even better. For military and PTSD, in one major study of 60,000 Iraq and Afghanistan veterans, 13.5 percent of deployed and not deployed veterans screened positive for PTSD, while other studies show the rate to be as high as 20 percent to 30 percent. As many as 500,000 US troops who served in these wars over the past thirteen years have been diagnosed with PTSD. These statistics are just based on two wars that the United States has been into and have been rather recent as compared to the traditional warriors that we might speak about.

Now, about entrepreneurs, according to the website Entrepreneur, in 2015, Michael A. Freeman, MD, from the University of California, San Francisco and his team researched mental health concerns among entrepreneurs. They found that 72 percent of the entrepreneurs surveyed reported mental health concerns. Specifically, 49 percent reported having one or more lifetime mental health conditions. Overall, entrepreneurs were 30 percent more likely to experience depression than members of the general population.

Entrepreneurs live in the *zone of the unknown*, unable to predict when and where ideas will pick up and turn into sustainable businesses. They have to continually test and question the value of what they have to offer. They become regular consumers of negative feedback. Their life is full of small failures. The funding didn't come through, the potential client didn't call back, the article didn't get published, the focus group didn't like the concept, and the family trip has to be canceled for lack of funds.

Yes, failure is an integral part of success. Successful people say so, failing people say so, gurus say so, and inspirational quotes say so. But dealing with mistakes, complaints, and rejection on a regular basis could make even the strongest self-esteem crumble—especially when that self-esteem becomes synonymous with being successful.

Entrepreneurs make huge emotional investments in their ideas: fully immersing themselves with their concepts, services, and gadgets. Their business becomes their identity. Any loss or failure is no longer just about time and money. It is about their self-worth. When this self-worth gets challenged, problems arise.

As we move forward, we must look into a couple of entrepreneurs who have fought mental illnesses and emerged better, stronger, and healthier to a certain extent. Their work has flourished, and so have they in this case. The first case in point would be Elon Musk. The guy is just never out of the news for something or the other that he either invents or invests into. Tesla CEO Elon Musk's life is the epitome of success for millions of young entrepreneurs. The serial entrepreneur recently opened up about his secret battle with depression. While replying to questions from other Twitter users about his mental state, Musk shared in a tweet, "The reality is great highs, terrible lows and unrelenting stress. Don't think people want to hear about the last two." Later, in a series of tweets, Musk also admitted to suffering from bipolar disorder. Previously known as manic depression, a bipolar is a mental disorder that causes periods of depression and periods of abnormally elevated mood.

Another entrepreneur we can take as an example here would be none other than one of the most popular and successful female-owned fashion brands in the United States, Kate Spade. Even though she the stresses over her business coupled with untreated depression caused her to spend too much time in the abyss and she eventually committed suicide. Her life and struggles have always kept her at the forefront of being targeted and hit by the likes of mental illnesses. Though she fought valiantly, it turned out to be a losing battle; her husband claimed her death was a result of her prolonged battle with depression and anxiety. The reason for mentioning one entrepreneur making it out of mental illnesses, while the other, despite fighting them like a warrior, giving in, is to show that if we take the right steps at the right time, mental health concerns can be tackled by warriors as well as entrepreneurs.

WHAT CAN YOU DO?

That is where the next question comes up. So, what do we do to ensure our mental well-being when looking into being successful entrepreneurs? Well, here are a few things that you can end up doing.

TAKE CARE OF YOUR BODY

Our bodies and minds are connected with one another. If we keep our bodies healthy, our brain and thought processes, too, get healthier and better. This includes regular exercising, eating all the right foods, and keeping an eye on alcohol intake. Anything! Just following a balanced diet with some regular exercise should be good enough here.

SEEK MEDICAL HELP

This is one of the most important things to do whenever you feel like you are mentally getting weakened or when you feel like the symptoms of any mental issue are starting to creep in on you. When you begin to do that, you will always have a professional's advice and help to guide you through. This help might include lifestyle changes, thinking pattern changes, and even medication. In all cases, it is important to look into medical help and take their educated opinion to work on yourselves.

REFLECT

Whenever you find yourself in a situation where things get mentally taxing, a great way to calm yourself down is to step back just a little bit and take a breather. As you take that breather, reflect on the ways that you are living your life. Reflect on the way that you think and the path that you have chosen for yourself. Is this path going to give you peace? Are you in a position to take the risks that you are taking with your mental health? These, amongst others, must be your questions in mind as you reflect and think things through.

CONNECT WITH OTHERS

As workaholics, people tend to isolate themselves, even when in working spaces. There is barely ever a need to do that. Yet we are all guilty of it, and there is no one to blame for that, not even ourselves. One way to cut down on that isolation could be to connect with others around you—be it fellow colleagues, or people who work in the same office building as you, or even making a good public relations rapport. Connect with people around you; you will find solace in that.

ALLOW YOUR FAMILY AND FRIENDS IN

This one is a no-brainer. There can be no better support than friends and family, and when things begin to go downhill, it is only fair for you to fall back upon the people you love and trust. Of course, you will need to give a significant amount of time and effort to the work you are doing, but whenever you feel mentally weak, know that people love you and would love to hear you out. It could be a rant about how tough the work is or just a simple support system. Basically, it is just having what you need!

With this, we come to the end of this journey that we took together through these pages of lesson, stories and research.

As your fellow warrior, I'm honored to know that others out there are willing to work hard, overcome challenges and embrace the warrior's way. We are all in this together, let's look out for each other. You never know the battles our brothers and sisters are experiencing as warriors typically don't ask for help. The warrior's journey is difficult but to the victor goes the spoils. Being an entrepreneurial warrior means taking time out of your life to do what most people won't so you can spend the rest of your life living like most others would never experience. Always remember that the journey can be as important as the end goal. Failure is never permanent, and neither is success. Learn from your challenges and failures, and help others on their journey. At the end of the day, the warrior is in the arena; everyone else is just a spectator.

"It is not the critic who counts; not the man who points out how the strong man stumbles, or where the doer of deeds could have done them better. The credit belongs to the man who is actually in the arena, whose face is marred by dust and sweat and blood; who strives valiantly; who errs, who comes short again and again, because there is no effort without error and shortcoming; but who does actually strive to do the deeds; who knows great enthusiasms, the great devotions; who spends himself in a worthy cause; who at the best knows in the end the triumph of high achievement, and who at the worst, if he fails, at least fails while daring greatly, so that his place shall never be with those cold and timid souls who neither know victory nor defeat."

—THEODORE ROOSEVELT, "MAN IN THE ARENA" SPEECH

ACKNOWLEDGEMENTS

———

So many people have helped me on my warrior's journey that if I listed everyone, this acknowledgements section would be longer than this book. I would be remiss if I didn't first thank my mom and dad, Jane and Barry. Their love, commitment to my happiness, and ensuring that I left home on the right trajectory is more than I anybody ever have wished for. You don't choose your parents, and I have been truly blessed to be fortunate enough to be born to such wonderful ones. I know I may have not been the best-behaved kid growing up—I still swear the beer keg hidden behind the pool table was not mine (it was actually my brother Adam's and stepbrother Rich's). We certainly put the "fun" in the dysfunctional family. I was also fortunate to have two wonderful stepparents in my life, Mary and Ward, who also helped ensure our entire family was surrounded by love, encouragement, and support. It was never us versus them, it was always just us.

I would like to thank (and apologize to) the teachers and staff of Roger Bacon High School. You gave me the support I needed along with the appropriate discipline to shape me into the man I am today. I would like to particularly thank my wrestling coaches and teachers Tom Roebel and Dan Starkey. Principal Fr. Jim Bok and my guidance counselor Sandra Farris taught me the true meaning of Franciscan love and compassion. As a matter of fact, if it wasn't for Mrs. Farris explaining to my English teacher that he would be stuck with me for summer school if he didn't move my F to a D, I probably would have never graduated. Mr. Chuck Grosser was the Dean of Discipline at Roger Bacon and many afternoons were spent in detention (JUG) where he helped "guide" me on the right track. Although I may not have appreciated him at the time, he certainly helped "smooth" out my "rough" edges (like my earring and mullet that he sent me home for on my first day of school).

I would also like to recognize my fraternity Sigma Phi Epsilon, Ohio Kappa Chapter at Bowling Green State University. My fraternity brothers made college more meaningful and enjoyable at the same time giving me the opportunity to learn to be a leader. One of my brothers Bill Evick and his wife Beth have remained dear friends. Bill is one of the people who inspired me to become an entrepreneur and do my best to follow in his successful footsteps.

My next-door neighbor, Tom Anderle, and his son Eric have not only been practically part of our family for over thirty years, but they have also always provided sound wisdom on my entrepreneurial journey. My best friend since I was in fourth grade is Oliver Stolley. We spent virtually every weekend at each other's house growing up. Be it playing hockey, GI Joe, or chasing girls, we have been inseparable. We made a pact at a very young age that we would both join the military, and not only did we honor that pact, but I am also proud to say he recently achieved the rank of Lieutenant Colonel in the US Army. -FYFH

I would like to thank my wife and son, Jennifer and Bryce. You two have been my inspiration to always do more, care more and try harder. You both have made sacrifices to support me on my warrior journey and without your love, support and encouragement, I would never have been able to make it this far. You are my rocks, and I love you dearly.

Finally, I would like to thank all of you who supported me in the funding of this book. You have all played a critical role in allowing *Warrior Entrepreneur* to be self-published, and I am grateful for your generosity and support.

Those people are as follows:

Adam, Heather, Miles and Tessa Green
Alexander Yastrebenetsky
Andrea Distasi
Barry Green
Brandon Niederschmidt
Casey Cooper
Cassandra Contreras
Christa Criddle
Christina Vest
Constance Maccarone
Craig Whelden
Cynthia Tucker
Danielle Mayoras/The Mayoras Family
David and Stacy Keszei
Debbie Dent

Deneen Wolber
Dennis Ramsey
Dianne K Rabe
Dom Santoleri
Elizabeth Edwards
Elizabeth Hartsock
Emily Seeskin
Eric Koester
Erin Neal
Gina Macarone and Zulfi Sharif
Jane and Ward Wenstrup
Jeff Wolber
Jennifer Green
Jennifer Sword
Jesse Dunbar
Judah Mitchell
Julie Dever
Karen Krieger
Laura Beasley
Lisa White
Lori Levy
Lynn Tetley
Mark Shuman
Mary Tarbell-Green
Michael Rumble
Michael Snyder
Mike Blaut
Mindy Green
Neal Hoffman
Nedra Ward
Neil Ursic
Nicola and Elisa Fontanive

Robert Holt
Roger Heldman
Sandra Rupp
Susan Chin
Suveer Shekhawat
Suzanne and Kevin Edwards
Tekkla Dana
Thaddeus Thorne
Tod Sackella
Zechariah King

APPENDIX

———

CHAPTER 2—MY STORY

"COVID-19 Mortality Rate for Intubated Adults Lower Than Previously Reported." *Respiratory Medicine* (June 10, 2020). https://www.practiceupdate.com/content/covid-19-mortality-rate-for-intubated-adults-lower-than-previously-reported/102029.

Danielson, Melissa L., Rebecca H. Bitsko, Reem M. Ghandour, Joseph R. Holbrook, Michael D. Kogan & Stephen J. Blumberg. "Prevalence of Parent-Reported ADHD Diagnosis and Associated Treatment Among U.S. Children and Adolescents." *Journal of Clinical Child & Adolescent Psychology* 47:2 (Jan. 24, 2018): 199-212. DOI: 10.1080/15374416.2017.1417860.

CHAPTER 3—THE WARRIOR SPIRIT

Massey Ratings Mascot database. Accessed June 29, 2021. www.masseyratings.com.

CHAPTER 4—THE SCIENCE OF ADVERSITY

McCorry, Laurie Kelly. "Physiology of the Autonomic Nervous System." *American Journal of Pharmaceutical Education* 71(4), 78 (2007). https://www.ncbi.nlm.nih.gov/pmc/articles/PMC1959222/.

CHAPTER 7—TEAMWORK

Check out the Entrepreneur Operating System at www.eosworldwide.com for more information on these concepts.

CHAPTER 10—TENACITY

"The Home Depot Announces Fourth Quarter and Fiscal 2020 Results; Increases Quarterly Dividend By 10 Percent." The Home Depot, February 23, 2021. https://corporate.homedepot.com/newsroom/news-release-home-depot-announces-fourth-quarter-2020-results.

CHAPTER 15—MORALITY

"Aquinas' Moral, Political, and Legal Philosophy." Stanford Encyclopedia of Philosophy. First published Fri Dec 2, 2005; substantive revision Tue Mar 16, 2021. https://plato.stanford.edu/entries/aquinas-moral-political/.

CHAPTER 16—SERENITY

Bray, R. M., Camlin, C. S., Fairbank, J. A., Dunteman, G. H., & Wheeless, S. C. The Effects of Stress on Job Functioning of Military Men and Women. *Armed Forces and Society*, 27(3) (2001): 397–417. https://doi.org/10.1177/0095327X0102700304.

Reisman, Miriam. "PTSD Treatment for Veterans: What's Working, What's New, and What's Next." *P & T: A Peer-reviewed Journal for Formulary Management*, 41(10) (2016): 623–634. https://www.ncbi.nlm.nih.gov/pmc/articles/PMC5047000/.